IT Leadership Manual

IT Leadership Manual

Roadmap to Becoming a Trusted Business Partner

ALAN R. GUIBORD

WILEY

John Wiley & Sons, Inc.

Library of Congress Cataloging-in-Publication Data:

Guibord, Alan R., 1947–
    IT leadership manual : roadmap to becoming a trusted business partner / Alan R. Guibord.
      p. cm.
    Includes bibliographical references and index.
    ISBN 978-1-118-11988-4 (cloth); ISBN 978-1-118-22466-3 (ebk);
    ISBN 978-1-118-26271-9 (ebk); ISBN 978-1-118-23796-0 (ebk)
  1. Information technology–Management.   2. Leadership.   I. Title.
    HD30.2.G85 2012
    658.4′038—dc23

                                    2012022659

Printed in the United States of America

10 9 8 7 6 5 4 3 2 1

This book is dedicated to my wife, Donna. Without her dedication and unwavering support, I would never have been able to achieve my goals.

Contents

Foreword

So you want to be a successful IT leader, eh? Well, you made a good start by picking up this book, because a lot of great IT technical people really suck at leadership skills. Moving from being an IT expert to a successful leader is really quite elusive and requires a hybrid blend of "hard skills" and "soft skills." There are plenty of textbooks on the technology that will take you to the glass ceiling of a career as a subject-matter expert, but there are not many books that focus on the "soft skills" specific to an IT role. So if you want to break through that glass ceiling, read on.

Leaders are not necessarily born but are molded and developed based on life's experiences. This book is designed to help guide each of us in our transitional journey to becoming effective leaders. We are all different in our personalities as well as our backgrounds. There is no one size that fits all. We each need to develop a style that works for of us. This book is designed to help us with that journey.

During the past 30 years, the focus in business was generally on improving operations, improving efficiencies, and building hierarchical organizations. This trend probably started back at the end of the industrial era and continued well into the '70s and '80s. Once we reached the '90s, things began to change; the focus became more and more on people and process where the way that people were led and motivated significantly changed. This phenomenon has continued to expand throughout the decade of the '90s and into the 2000s. We are now at a point in the business world where it's more about how we lead than how we execute. Leadership has become the primary competitive advantage in today's world. During the past few decades there was very little focus on developing effective leaders. That has now changed in today's world with the advent of the Internet and other global communications capabilities that have transformed us into a global economy and a global business environment. We no longer have the luxury of having our entire staff located in one or two physical facilities. Today's world is virtual in every way. It is virtual in the services that we provide as well as the organizations that we manage. The only way that we can effectively address this new world is through developing better leaders.

During my over-30-year career in corporate life I've witnessed this phenomenon firsthand. There has been a definite shift in focus from the world of efficiency and productivity to one of people and process. This requires a new type of leader and I have personally experienced the journey of transition in my own style as well. We now live in a world with an abundance of outside sources of information and stimuli. These have a tremendous amount of impact on our day-to-day lives and the way we approach our personal and business lives. We need to recognize the influence that these factors have on our behavior as we adjust our leadership style.

So much has changed in recent memory—the way we communicate, the way we interact with each other, and the multi-generations in the workforce all lend themselves to the need to create a new model. I have always prided myself on being people-centric throughout my career, and that didn't always sit well with my consuming interest in technology innovation. I had to push myself to face the fact that the demands on leaders today are far different than they were even 10 years ago. It means that we are now in a world of personalization and instant gratification thanks to the advent of the Internet. It's now all about personal relationships rather than group dynamics. The way that we lead and motivate needs to be aligned with these new phenomenons.

I strongly believe that this book should be required reading for every aspiring leader. It's very easy for all of us to say, "I don't have the time to work on these soft skills due to the day-to-day demands that are being placed on me." What this book makes you aware of is the fact that each and every one of us must allocate a substantial amount of our personal time in learning how to develop enhance and improve our leadership skills.

The book also teaches us about being aware of the world in general. Not just the workplace but the entire environment in which we live. We can no longer separate our lives into two areas: one in which we work and one in which we live. This new environment now requires us to develop a single style of leadership. It requires us to build on strong relationships and personal experiences. These are behavioral characteristics that can be consciously developed, but you have to be as structured about developing your soft skills as you have been about developing your hard skills. Alan has taken the time to articulate his wise counsel and offer a roadmap for each of you to follow as you develop your unique personal leadership style.

Jim Noble
Senior Vice President, Talisman Energy Inc.

Preface

I t is a warm summer day at Watkins Glen International Raceway. I am just finishing my second test session of the day. It is unusually hot for this time of year and we have had to make several adjustments to the car. I am here as part of the F2000 Championship Series, a professional series in its sixth year.

Young kids from all over the world are here, and the competition is tougher every year. With over 30 cars competing, there are only two seconds separating the field. Every one-hundredth of a second is important.

We have made several adjustments to the chassis, added new springs, adjusted the Penske shocks, played with ride height, and adjusted tire pressures. Our team engineer, Angello, calls a racecar "the unsolvable equation." He has a degree in mechanical engineering and is a great asset to the team. He can prepare each car to the individual driver's preferences. I like understeer, which we call "a push." It causes the front end to be a little loose. The advantage to me is that it keeps the rear more stable. Every driver has his own style.

The young drivers like our series because it features several experienced drivers. Many are national champions. We range in age from 17 to 72. I love to watch the kids learn and grow from our mentorship. All they know is how to go fast, but speed is not the only thing that counts. It is all about how you enter a turn and how you pick your turning and breaking points. It might be a tree, a spot in the track, a bump, or any other recognizable object that you can identify at over 100 MPH. Every new racer makes the same two mistakes: turning in too early and carrying too much speed into the corner. This leaves the driver fighting with the car when he should be accelerating out of the turn. Young drivers eventually learn from following us and we love to mentor them.

Driving a racecar is a constant battle between your mind and the car. The car is telling you it can make it through that corner faster and your mind is telling you it can't. This is probably one of the most difficult things for drivers to overcome. If you don't, you will never be fast. You develop the feel of your body moving inside the car and soon you can translate that into knowing the limits of the car. Like people, each car has a personality; like people, we must treat each car as an individual.

We have a three-car team; myself, my son, Alan, and our friend Bob. We have been together for over 10 years. During that time, we have learned one another's strengths and weaknesses. When we go out, we follow each other to learn what each of us is doing in certain parts of the track. We also have video cameras as well as computer telemetry on each car. During qualifying, we take turns leading while the others get in behind and push the leader. I must say that I am a better racer than a qualifier. I am always overdriving the car.

When we return to the pits, we immediately download our computer telemetry as well as the video chips. Then we all go to the trailer lounge, the whole team. We overlay the data to see where each one is faster and slower. We then compare it to the videos to gain an understanding of what we are doing. The camera does not lie. If you are not hitting your marks, it will show you. After we have all shared the computer data and watched the video, we provide individual feedback as to how we feel the car is performing.

The things I like most about racing are the competition, the team, and the camaraderie. We have two rules: (1) Don't beat them in the pits, which means help your fellow competitor when he or she is struggling with a broken car, and (2) we all have to go to work on Monday. I think you understand that last one. Enough said.

Teamwork is the key to success in racing as well as business. The principles are the same. Maybe it is just a little more intense at the track. We succeed and fail together. Each person has his or her designated assignment. If one fails to deliver, we all fail.

Keeping your team motivated is critical to winning. When your team spends countless hours preparing your car and you put it into the wall on the first lap, it can be devastating. It is all about how you handle it with them when you get back to the pits. The first thing you do is apologize. The second thing you do is talk about what went wrong. The third thing you do is roll up your sleeves and help to fix it. Remember all the time that each member has an assignment. Offer assistance, but let each member of the team do his or her job. Let your team know that you respect their contributions.

Leading and motivating a team is crucial to winning. They need to know that you appreciate them. They need to be proud of their efforts. Your job is to assist when needed, provide the tools and physical setting, and give them motivation and reinforcement. Done right, a team is like a well-orchestrated performance. This is true in business as well.

I have learned many lessons from my days at the track. These experiences, and the lessons they provide about competition, teamwork, and leadership have provided the foundation for my career. I will be sharing these lessons with you throughout the book.

The book is designed to help you create your own personal journey to becoming a trusted leader. The process begins with a self-evaluation. This exercise is designed to help you create an objective look at your inner being. It is a critical building block on your journey. The next step is to start planning your career path. In order to understand your personal needs, you must first set personal career goals. These will then become the foundation for your personal plan. This is not a one-time effort, but a continual exercise as you move through your career.

The next three chapters are designed to be a guide to developing your personal leadership style. There is no one-size-fits-all when it comes to leadership. It must be a balance of the basic fundamentals molded to your personal comfort zone. This again is something that you will be continually revisiting throughout your career.

Once you have completed your self-evaluations, it is now time to start building your skills. Chapter 7 on relationships is, in my opinion, one of the most important aspects of becoming a trusted partner. It is all about people working with people and this chapter is designed to help you to recognize your own approach, but also, to impress on you the need for being a strong relationship builder. Leadership is all about balance and in Chapter 8 I have provided you with some thought-provoking ideas as well as recommendations for living a balanced life. It is impossible to achieve your goals without personal balance.

Leadership is also about influencing the behavior of others. The best way is to hone your sales skills. Selling your concepts and ideas is critical to gaining trust and respect. You can't ignore the need to sell. Many of us dislike the thought of having to sell. However, it is critical to our success. The higher you go in an organization, the more you will need to hone your selling skills. Chapter 9 is designed to first make you aware of the need to sell and then how to learn to sell based on your personality.

In today's world, changing jobs is a part of life. Most IT leaders change jobs every three to five years. We need to understand how to effectively integrate ourselves into new organizations and cultures. In Chapter 10, I have shared my own experiences as well as those of others to help you better prepare for your next change.

The last chapter, Chapter 11, is about dealing with the new world we now live in. The pace of change continues to accelerate and we now must accept it as part of our daily lives. In addition, new technologies such as the Internet have had a profound effect on our lives and the way we work with others. The market is also looking for a whole new set of skills and we now must understand what the market is looking for and fill our personal gaps to align with them. The last chapter is designed to address those topics as well as bring all the concepts of the book together.

Acknowledgments

I thank the following for making this book possible:

My children, Sandra and Alan. Their love and support have always been my inspiration.

My racing teammates. We have had quite a ride and I cherish the memories. Drive fast and take chances!

My corporate friends. There are too many to identify each one, but, my thanks to all of you for joining me in the journey.

My mentors, Bob Goundry and Howard Hosbach. The lessons I learned from them gave me the courage to take on challenges with confidence and conviction.

IT Leadership Manual

CHAPTER 1

The Journey

Today's Leadership Challenges

This book presents insights I have gained as a business professional for over 35 years and from my experiences as a racecar driver. The lessons I have learned in the boardroom and in the driver's seat have been the key to my personal leadership growth. Being a leader is about more than your experience in the workplace—it is about the way you conduct your life and the lessons you learn from your life experiences.

In racing, driving the car is the smallest part of the effort required to compete successfully. By far the largest part of that effort is your preparation for a race and your ability to collaborate with your crew and your team. Leadership is about building a team that you can work with, developing trust among the members of your team, and sharing your successes. It is about knowing how to get the most out of every personal relationship and developing the interpersonal skills necessary to address any situation you encounter. Becoming a trusted leader is about developing the self-knowledge, experience, and skills that serve as a foundation of your personal leadership style. This foundation provides you with the comfort and confidence others seek in a leader. The social, economic, and corporate climates have changed dramatically over the last few decades. Leaders today need to develop an entirely new set of skills to effectively perform in all three of those arenas. Leadership today is more about personal relationships and your personal comfort zones than ever before; in the chapters that follow, I discuss how to build strong personal relationships and expand your comfort zone to prepare you for the challenges facing leaders today.

> Being a leader is about more than your experience in the workplace; being a leader is about the way you conduct your life and the lessons you learn from your life experiences.

Throughout the book, I stress that leadership is personal and not something you can learn by studying a business textbook. Personal knowledge, combined with your experiences and relationships, is the foundation on which today's successful leaders build. Developing a personal leadership style with which you are comfortable is the key to meeting the many challenges you will face throughout your life. You need to develop a style that is consistent with your unique ideals and aspirations—you can't stray too far from who you are. To be successful as a leader, you need to be at peace with yourself and operate in your personal comfort zone. Leadership is not about being flamboyant and overly expressive; it is about building the best model for you. I talk often throughout the book about things like how self-evaluation, understanding your leadership style, and learning from personal experience can help you become a more effective leader. I also offer examples from experiences in my personal, business, and racing lives.

One of the largest hurdles to becoming an effective leader and business partner is building trust, and the same holds true in racing. When you are about to be strapped into a car that you will drive at over 140 miles an hour you need to have the utmost trust in your crew team and the faith that they have done their job and prepared your car so it is not only competitive but safe. This type of trust does not come easily; it takes years to build, through multiple experiences both good and bad. While the immediate consequences are less dire, trust in your team is just as important in corporate life. No matter what the situation, it is impossible to be a strong leader without trust. People are people whether you encounter them at a racetrack or in an office. We all have similar motivations, aspirations, prejudices, and experiences. What I attempt to do in this book is help to guide you through your personal journey—to help you understand more about yourself, your surroundings, and your reactions to the world. This understanding will help you establish the foundation on which to build your own personal leadership style.

> Direct personal interaction with others is the glue that holds people together, and to succeed as a leader you must use personal interaction to build trust and bind people to one another.

One of the themes of this book is the importance of building strong personal relationships. Without them, it is impossible to be effective in your personal or business endeavors. We have more ways to communicate today than ever before, but many of the methods available to us—such as text messages, e-mail, and voicemail—are impersonal. Despite the ease of these communication methods, direct personal interaction with others is the glue that holds people together, and to succeed as a leader you must use personal interaction to build trust and bind people to one another. I place a high value on making direct personal contact whenever possible. I will sometimes drive several hours just for a one-hour meeting so I can have that personal interaction with someone. You can learn so much when you deal face-to-face with others that a little extra effort on your part can be handsomely rewarded. When you meet someone in person, you have an opportunity to learn from facial expressions, body language, and tone of voice in a way that is not currently possible through the different types of electronic communication available to us. We live in a global world, and it can be difficult for us to always interact personally; however, you should take the opportunity to engage in personal interaction whenever possible. One of the tools I use a lot when I am not able to meet someone in person is videoconferencing. There are very inexpensive means today—including Skype and other technologies—that allow you to capture some of the elements of personal interaction that are missing in many types of digital communication. Videoconferencing allows you to directly observe the reactions of the person with whom you are conversing, both the obvious reactions and the subtle physical cues of face and gesture that are essential to understanding others' responses. Speaking face-to-face, even when you are miles apart, also helps you build stronger personal bonds than correspondence alone. Never forget the importance of human interaction; very few lasting achievements are accomplished by an individual. To succeed today, you must be part of a successful team.

> One of the themes of this book is the importance of building strong personal relationships.

The New World Order and the IT Challenge

Becoming an effective leader today is more challenging than ever before. The expectations continue to change; however, the basic principles remain the same. In this book I will help you understand the challenges involved in becoming a leader and suggest how you can develop a personal plan to help improve your leadership skills. There is no one-size-fits-all model when it comes to leadership. Your leadership style is an individual approach based on your personal beliefs, values, and desires. Becoming a leader is about developing your style such that you are comfortable with yourself and with the environment around you. Many people understand leadership too narrowly. Leadership requires more than supervising others; it is an approach to your day-to-day activities in all areas of your life. Leadership involves building relationships and learning to cope with situations throughout your life. In ways large and small, each of us practices the skills required of successful leaders every day; one of the goals of this book is to help you recognize this so you can practice those skills more meaningfully.

The leadership challenges facing an IT (information technology) organization today are different than those facing other areas of business. IT people, by nature, tend to be very analytical, very calculated, and very process-driven. In addition, many IT people tend to have an introverted personality. Much like engineers, IT people are more focused on the job at hand rather than worrying about the larger picture. This is a major hurdle that we need to overcome in order to develop effective leadership skills. Most other areas of business have much more daily interaction with multiple organizational departments. For example, finance personnel tend to work regularly with people from every department in a corporation. Although IT supports activities across the entire company, many IT personnel avoid having regular interaction with people outside the IT department. This restricts the interpersonal development necessary to success. Anyone hoping to rise to a leadership role must consider interaction with people across the company as an integral part of his or her daily routine.

The IT organization in most corporations today always seems troubled by the need to justify its existence; IT leaders often struggle to be perceived as true business partners. I've heard complaints for decades now from executives who believe the IT organization is not aligned with the business. I also hear from many chief executive officers who understand that they need IT but don't understand why. There has been a value creation void in IT organizations for several decades and now is the time for us to close that gap. We need to break old habits of viewing IT as distinct from other areas of the business and work actively to integrate technology into the business in a way that provides obvious identifiable value to powerbrokers throughout the company. We need to shift our focus to identifying and measuring the business value created by IT efforts. We need to do a better job requiring up-front benefit identification for new projects. IT efforts need to be business-generated and business-owned. Clearly articulated benefit delivery is also a must. Benefits must have four clear requirements: (1) how much, (2) how delivered, (3) who is responsible for delivery, and (4) over what timeframe. The best way to become a trusted leader is to consistently create quantifiable value within the business. Having a defined delivery mechanism is the only way to achieve consistent success.

While IT leaders need to revisit their approach to working with other areas of the business, corporations also need to change their approach to IT in order to address the historical lack of understanding and support for IT efforts. Past generations of IT leaders have risen primarily through the technical ranks. They were thrust into leadership positions because they were unable to move beyond a particular salary limit working as a programmer, an analyst, or a computer operator. A desire to advance their careers forced them to move into management roles that demanded a type of leadership that was new to people used to technical work. Many of them were put into these roles with very little training and little background in the leadership skills necessary to success. Even today, many organizations still fail to provide IT leaders the support necessary for them to develop their leadership skills.

> We need to break old habits of viewing IT as distinct from other areas of the business and work actively to integrate technology into the business in a way that provides obvious identifiable value to powerbrokers throughout the company.

As IT leaders, we are entrusted with significant amounts of corporate money every year; however, business leaders in other areas of the corporation often fail to fully understand the business and technological hurdles IT must overcome to invest those funds effectively. Because business leaders never clearly understand IT as well as other areas of the company, such as manufacturing, accounting, and sales, they are less comfortable when things go wrong. Problems that seem manageable in other areas of the company are seen as major crises when they happen to assets managed by IT. This unease arises because business leaders must trust IT to make the right decisions when faced with questions most people do not understand. For decades now, corporations have had to trust us with their investments, but we need to change the game. We need to strike out and become the leaders corporations have always hoped we would be. We need to take charge of ourselves and our destinies.

In today's world, corporations have a whole new set of expectations for IT leaders. They now expect us to be visionaries, collaborators, and innovators. What companies today need are business leaders who understand technology rather than the technologists who understand something about the business who previously ran IT departments. One of the focuses of this book is the need for today's IT leaders to first develop an intimate understanding of the corporations for which they work and, second, build the strongest possible personal relationships they can at all levels within the corporation. The only way we can overcome the failings of the past is to move boldly to the future. The objective of this book is to provide guidelines for becoming the IT leaders corporations have been expecting us to be for decades.

After you understand the expectations of today's corporations and the need to build the strong personal relationships, it becomes very easy for you and your organization to align with the business in a way that IT organizations have been unable to in the past. Alignment is about gaining the confidence of your peers, reassuring them that you have a full understanding of their needs and requirements, and building a trusting relationship with them so they know you can effectively translate business needs into technology solutions that vastly improve the corporation. This is how you overcome the hurdle presented by a lack of confidence and business alignment. I write at length about tools and aids that will help you develop your own personal leadership style to achieve these ends.

> One of the focuses of this book is the need for today's IT leaders to first develop an intimate understanding of the corporations for which they work and, second, build the strongest possible personal relationships they can at all levels within the corporation.

Today's Cultures

There are also several cultural challenges to becoming a leader in today's environment. Like it or not, we all live in a global community. We no longer have the luxury of planning our business and economic cycles in a vacuum. Business concerns of U.S. corporations are now intertwined with those of corporations from every other country in the world. This has caused a complete shift in the way decisions are made and in the way organizations are built and led. A whole new style needs to be developed to address the challenges presented by today's interconnected world.

It sometimes seems as though we are riding a treadmill and being forced to make decisions for increasingly shorter terms. In this environment, it becomes a challenge to build strong relationships; however, personal relationships are more necessary today than ever before. In order to become an effective leader in today's environment, we need to be able to embrace multiple cultures, backgrounds, and experiences. Leadership is no longer about leading a team in your specific geographical area whose members share a similar background and culture. Instead, you must adapt your leadership style to the multiple cultures of your team and find ways to use their backgrounds and experiences as assets rather than liabilities. The advent of the Internet and other associated technologies has made the world a smaller and smaller place. You can no longer isolate yourself from this phenomenon. The United States, indeed, the world, is moving toward a new cultural environment where a new world cultural order is emerging from the mixing and matching of various cultures we have been performing for two or three generations now. We need to recognize that in order to be effective as leaders and as individuals in this new multicultural society we have to be adept at modifying our thought processes and our behaviors so we can effectively coexist with these many cultures. Today's leaders have found ways to adjust their behavior and their thoughts and actions in order to accommodate this new reality. We now need to be much more open-minded and receptive to change that we ever have been before and accept that this new world order means we are part of a larger community. This change cannot be ignored.

> You must adapt your leadership style to the multiple cultures of your team and find ways to use their backgrounds and experiences as assets rather than liabilities.

Over the next few generations, we will be moving closer and closer to one common culture and one common language; we can see this shift already. I was riding a train to New York City a few years ago and a Hispanic woman and her daughter were sitting in the seat next to me. I listened to them converse and was surprised at what I heard. They were not speaking in Spanish or in English but in a combination of the two languages. That overheard conversation made it evident to me that language barriers will be less of an obstacle for future generations as technology and freedom of movement move us toward a common language and culture. You must be prepared for this type of shift in culture and language as you build your leadership style because this trend is likely to shape the cultural landscape for decades to come. We need to be cognizant of the changes in the way business is conducted throughout the world and adjust our behavior and actions such that we are continually in tune with the migration of ideas and practices among cultures. As you read this book and begin to develop your own personal leadership style, keep this point in mind as you think about the most effective ways you can adapt yourself and your day-to-day activities.

The differences between the cultural, philosophical, and idealistic visions of the multiple generations in today's workplace are more profound than ever before. In most corporations today, we are dealing with three generations—each with a unique set of objectives, desires, and motivations. Each one of these generations is totally different from the others in these aspects. My generation was not introduced to computers until we were in our early to mid-20s. The generation behind me was introduced to computers at a slightly earlier age—maybe in their teens. The current generation grew up with computers from the time they were two years old. Two or three years ago I was sitting in a restaurant lounge waiting for a table and a woman sat down next to me with her young son. As they waited for a table, she gave him her iPhone and he immediately picked it up and began playing with it. After observing her for a while I walked over and asked how old her son was—he was two and a half years old. I was flabbergasted to think that a child that age was already computer literate. This generational shift is a major challenge for us as leaders in today's world. Faced with multiple generations that have been introduced to technology at various points in their lives, we must address their different needs when they come together in the workplace. In order to be an effective leader in today's world we must now bridge the gap between these generations and create a functional leadership style in our organizations that not only allows them to coexist, but to complement one another. Dealing with multiple generations can present challenges as difficult to overcome as those presented by the need to deal with multiple cultural backgrounds.

The world is now looking for visionaries rather than people who can execute well. Efficiency and execution have been the mandates for several decades, but it is now time for us to develop a new level of awareness and understanding about the corporations that employ us. It is all about people first and products second. Without strong leadership and organizational structures that foster creativity and vision, companies will struggle to succeed in the future.

Objective of This Book

This book was written to help you develop the knowledge and skills that will allow you to become an effective and trusted leader in today's environment. It will also teach you how to build better relationships and develop an environment of trust with your peers and those above and below you in your company's hierarchy. It is essential that you look at the creation of a leadership style as a journey rather than as a structured set of predetermined steps you need to follow in order to achieve success.

I reiterate many times throughout the coming chapters that leadership requires you to develop an individual style, and the ultimate goal of this style is to allow you to comfortably build trust and influence the behavior of those around you. The industrial era as we know it has ended, and we have now moved into more of a professional services environment. There are no set standard operating procedures or manufacturing operation manuals to help us navigate this new world. We must learn to develop a style of our own that allows us to make the migration. Throughout the book, I include passages about specific experiences I have had; based on these experiences, I offer specific recommendations about how to develop a unique leadership style. The most important skill you can learn, though, is how to build strong personal relationships and develop a single approach to relationships in all areas of your life rather than trying to create separate business and personal personas. You will learn that in today's world it is important to develop an ability to influence others' behavior because mandating actions is a failing leadership strategy. You will also learn how to create organizations that are closely focused to the objectives of the business rather than individual technological requirements.

> The most important skill you can learn, though, is how to build strong personal relationships and develop a single approach to relationships in all areas of your life rather than trying to create separate business and personal personas.

The easiest way to learn is through the experience of others. My hope is that the experiences and ideas I share with you throughout the book will help you develop your leadership style without having to suffer the failures and mistakes of those of us who have come before you. There is no replacement for experience, and I try here to share experiences with you in the hope that you will take them, modify them, and use them as a foundation for your individual leadership development process. There is no one-size-fits-all path to leadership, but many of the challenges you face are not unique, and learning from the experiences of others in similar situations can prepare you to succeed. With any book, presentation, or speech, the audience never fully grasps all the concepts presented the first time through. My objective is to provide you with a set of ideas, observations, and suggestions that you can refer to regularly to help you as you build your own personal foundation for leadership. It is not an informational manual, but I hope it can give you some useful guidance for your personal journey.

Becoming an invested and trusted leader in today's environment is all about matching your personal skills and behaviors to the expectations of today's society. The greatest thing we can achieve in our lives is an honorable and trusted reputation. This is the legacy we leave behind. Success in life is not about the money or material things we acquire—it's the impression we make on others and, equally as important, the success others achieve through their relationships with us. Leadership is not a task be taken lightly. It needs to be a part of our daily lives and we need to understand the capabilities as well as the consequences of our actions. The objective of this book is, finally, to give you the tools to build that reputation for trustworthiness and take a leadership role in every area of your life.

CHAPTER 2

We Are All Unique

Many people ask me why I drive a racecar. Most people think I am crazy for doing so. I tell them I do it because it fits my personality. I am a driven person constantly setting goals and always trying to improve. This started at a very young age, and I can't explain why I am this way except to say that I had meager beginnings and always wanted to prove that I could beat the odds and excel. You don't have to be excessively driven to succeed; however, you must have a personal motivation to continuously challenge yourself. No two races and no two business situations are the same. What makes you successful is your personal preparedness and ability to adapt to unique situations. It all starts with learning about yourself.

At the time of this writing, I just finished giving a presentation on leadership in Atlanta—my third engagement this month. As always, I tried to read the audience. I watched body language and considered the questions audience members asked. When giving a presentation, I try to imagine myself in the audience. I want to make sure the information I provide is timely and relevant and that everyone will learn something of value. Then I try to season this valuable information with a pinch of entertainment. Today things seemed to go very well.

Public speaking did not come easily to me; it took many years of training and practice to reach the comfort level I enjoy today. Still, it is often a challenge to reconcile my inner feelings about speaking in public with the external persona I try to project when addressing a large crowd. Achieving this balance took efforts in the office, on the racetrack, and in all areas of my life, but it has been one of the keys to my success as a leader. My development as a leader began many years ago as the result of a personal self-evaluation. Successful self-evaluation is not easy to do unless you are completely honest with yourself, but I found it to be a very enlightening experience and it served as the starting line for my leadership career. This chapter summarizes key lessons I have learned throughout my career as a leader that can be applied by anyone with a sincere desire to improve and become an effective leader.

> The first step in becoming a trusted partner is to look within yourself and find out what makes you tick.

Look within Yourself First

The first step in becoming a trusted partner is to look within yourself and find out what makes you tick. What I mean by that is to identify what motivates you, where your comfort zones lie, how tolerant you are of others, and whether you are comfortable leading or following. We spend our entire lives evaluating others. We constantly size people up and try to understand what makes them tick, yet we spend very little time evaluating ourselves in this way. It is normal when speaking with someone to try to "read" that person. Many leaders brag that after years of corporate life they are able to size people up more easily than they were years ago. The wisdom that comes with experience helps us see people more clearly and weed out the good from the bad. This is something you can't get from a textbook; it grows from a combination of personal experiences and an understanding of yourself.

The most important element of becoming a trusted leader is to understand yourself. What makes you tick and what are your defining personal traits? You need to clearly understand yourself before you can attempt to understand others. Our perceptions are formed by our personalities. In order to be successful, you need to understand your core identity, and identify the behavioral changes you must make if you really want to take the next step in your career.

Self-Evaluation Process

The best way to begin a self-evaluation is to reflect on your personal preferences and impulses. What motivates you? What makes you happy? What makes you uneasy, nervous, or uncomfortable? Then, consider your position in relation to others. What are your responsibilities? What is your role? What is the scope of your influence on those around you? Now, compare your current position to experiences you have had in the past to see if you are currently in your comfort zone. After making this assessment, the next step is to seek input from others: people you trust, people you work with, people in your family, people in your neighborhood, people in your church. Ask them what it is that makes you a unique person. What is it about your personality that sets you apart and what areas do you need to improve. Make sure you ask them to be honest and explain that you are trying to gain a better understanding of yourself and you would greatly appreciate help with your journey. You don't need to seek professional help to do an adequate job evaluating yourself; the most important thing is being open-minded and honest with yourself in your evaluation.

> The best way to begin a self-evaluation is to reflect on your personal preferences and impulses.

Reading Others

Business is about personal interaction and negotiation. Having a clear understanding of yourself is the first step. The next is to learn to interact with others. The art of reading others, especially in a negotiation, is an important one for success in the corporate world. Many years ago, when I was beginning my career, an experienced negotiator taught me that when you are in a negotiation the first thing to do is try to understand where your opponent is coming from and discover what it will take to make him or her happy. The second thing to do is state your case, make your offer, and then be quiet. At that point, the first one to talk loses. This has worked well for me over the years, although I must tell you there have been several situations where I sat staring silently staring at the person across the table for long periods of time. This can be a very awkward situation; however, it usually works.

One time when I was purchasing a car I was in a heated negotiation about the price. I finally made an offer and told the salesman it was my final offer and he could take it or leave it. I then stopped talking. We went through about 30 agonizing seconds of complete quiet. It seemed like an eternity. When you take that posture, you back your opponent into a corner and the only way out is to accept or try for more negotiations. In either case, you have the upper hand and your opponent must now give ground. In this case, I got my price. Part of the process is acting convincing. If you can successfully convey a sense of seriousness, those around you are more likely to treat the matter seriously. It is a bit of a battle of nerves. I have experienced this many times in both my corporate and racing life. Holding your ground and letting someone know you are serious works well. Facial expression is also a great help. Don't be afraid to look right at someone with a serious look on your face.

Another key point in our interactions with others is that human nature causes us to want what we can't have. In Donald Trump's book *The Art of The Deal*, he includes a story about a manufacturer with products that were not selling to expectations, so the manufacturer created a waiting list for them.[1] This caused people to want the product more because it was suddenly unavailable to them. Many years ago, you could not get Coors beer east of the Rockies. At the time, I was traveling to Denver regularly and on each trip I would bring a couple of cases back with me. People would pay up to $50 per case just to have what they could not buy at home. After the beer became available nationally, the luxury went away and demand dropped off. When we interact with others, if we can find a way to create demand, it increases the value of our product. Try to find ways to create a sense of exclusivity wherever you can as a way to influence those around you. Also, try to be aware of your own motivations and understand the way in which others are reading and attempting to influence you.

Make Time for Yourself

In today's world, with its constant barrage of informational stimuli, very few of us ever take time to sit down and really think about ourselves, about who we are, and about what makes us tick. This type of self-assessment is not self-centered—it's an essential practice of those who are looking to improve. You need to understand your motivations and how they are shaped by your experiences. They both have a tremendous influence on your behavior and need to be clearly understood so you can make the most informed decisions possible. We get so consumed with our business responsibilities, with our family lives, with the bills, and with all the other day-to-day decisions we must make very quickly, that we forget the need to spend time understanding ourselves.

Throughout my years in corporate life, one thing has really kept me on track: I have always taken the time to examine myself on a daily basis and evaluate how I performed and how others might have perceived my actions. I think it is very important for all of us to do that, no matter how busy we may be. Many leaders have told me, "I just have no time in the day for me." You really must manage your time efficiently to be an effective leader in today's world. It is not just about sitting at your desk and working all day long. It is about recognizing the other priorities, both personal and interpersonal, that are just as important as accomplishing the tasks listed in your job description. We each must carve out portions of every day for specific activities. In addition to the time I set aside each day to reflect on my performance, I also allocate time for roaming— for walking the halls, meeting and talking with the staff in my organization, and checking in with my peers. Of course, I also allocate a certain amount of time to getting my work done.

> An important question to start with when performing a self-evaluation is whether or not you really want to become a leader.

An important question to start with when performing a self-evaluation is whether or not you really want to become a leader. We are all conditioned to feel that we should aspire to leadership positions in order to gain recognition and success. However, leadership means different things to different people and doesn't necessarily lead to these rewards. "Leadership" is a nebulous term. Each of us is unique in our experiences, thoughts, and perceptions; we each understand leadership differently, and we each have different motivations to become leaders. Understanding your feelings about leadership, particularly when moving into a new role, helps you understand whether that role fits within your comfort zone. Just as we all come from different backgrounds and from different life experiences, not all of us feel comfortable in leadership positions, just as not all of us feel comfortable standing in front of a room and giving a management-level presentation. Before you begin your move to the front office, take time to assess yourself. Develop an in-depth understanding of why you want to make this move. Take an inventory of what interests and excites you, and of past experiences that caused you to challenge yourself. For example, I always thought of myself as an introvert. I liked being alone and often felt uncomfortable in social interactions. However, when I interviewed people who'd known me many years, I found they perceived me as totally the opposite. They viewed me as someone who seemed comfortable in front of a crowd, who enjoyed the spotlight, and who liked being around people. This helped reveal an internal conflict I resolved by seeking out new challenges and leadership opportunities.

Honest self-evaluation is crucial to becoming a leader. Your understanding of your limitations, your comfort zones, the things at which you excel, and the things with which you struggle is the foundation of successful leadership. The best leaders I know have this intimate understanding of themselves and use that knowledge to address their weaknesses by surrounding themselves with people who can fill the gaps. Becoming a trusted business partner means making people understand you know where your place is, where their place is, and that you have taken the time to create an environment where you can both work together and take advantage of each other's strengths.

> Honest self-evaluation is crucial to becoming a leader.

Know What You Don't Know

I often tell people that good leaders know both what they know and what they don't know. Having said that, you need to have the courage to go out and fill gaps in your experience and interest with the best possible people you can find. Don't feel insecure when doing this. The reason most managers fail is because they are afraid to bring in people who have strengths to fill their gaps. It is human nature to think you can solve every problem and meet every challenge. The truth is that each of us has limitations. We all have things we do well and things we don't do well. Strong leaders are not afraid to find team members with the expertise to fill those gaps and use that expertise to help themselves grow as individuals. Weak leaders try to do it on their own and usually fail. Knowing this, we can now begin our journey. The importance of forming strong teams is covered in Chapter 4.

> Good leaders know both what they know and what they don't know. You need to have the courage to go out and fill gaps in your experience and interest with the best possible people you can find.

Journey to Self-Awareness

Conducting an accurate self-evaluation is one of the most difficult things for us to do, yet it is an important step in understanding the challenges we face as we prepare ourselves for leadership roles. It lets us understand ourselves and influence the way others perceive us. Perception is reality, and we must recognize how others perceive us as we begin our evaluative journey. Also, understanding the ways in which we act and react is critical to building strong relationships. I waited far too long to take the first crucial step of self-evaluation, and it cost me valuable time in my climb up the corporate ladder. The longer you delay, the more set in your ways you become, which makes it increasingly difficult to properly prepare for your career.

> Perception is reality, and we must recognize how others perceive us as we begin our evaluative journey.

The self-evaluation is the starting point for all of my executive-coaching engagements. It provides a strong footing upon which we can begin to build a leadership style. All too often we force ourselves into roles for which we are not prepared. And all too often, the result is that we do not succeed. Understanding your inner self helps you recognize and prepare for the many opportunities and challenges you will encounter.

Self-Awareness Exercise

Let's try an exercise that leads to a critical set of decisions. It allows you to determine the behaviors you are capable of changing and those you cannot change (accepting that behavioral change takes time and effort). Years ago I made the decision to change myself from an introvert to an extrovert and from a team player to a team leader. These were not easy adjustments for me to make, and to this day I still have to monitor my behavior. Such decisions cannot be taken lightly and, once you start this journey, it requires daily effort to continue.

Take a piece of paper and write down how you perceive yourself. Be specific. Are you an introvert or extrovert? Are you a driver or do you prefer to be driven? Are you compassionate? How long is your attention span? How do you deal with authority? What is your leadership style? Are you passionate? How do you display your moods? Be honest; don't describe the person you'd like to be. Look at yourself objectively.

Now, create a graph of your findings. On the vertical axis measure comfort and on the horizontal axis list the activities and actions you included in your evaluation. Complete honesty is essential to success, so think carefully about your graph and how you measure each item on it. On the horizontal axis list all the activities you consider important to becoming an effective leader. Things like building relationships, giving presentations, making decisions, and any others required for success in your current and future leadership roles. Use this graph as your personal reference point. Your graph might look like the following example when you are done.

Comfort Level

	Presenting to others	Negotiating	Networking with peers	Talking on the phone	Dealing with conflict	Leading conversations	Being the center of attention	Introducing new concepts	Listening and talking	Meeting new people at events	Entertaining new concepts
High											
Medium											
Low											

What I like to do is create the graph and throughout my career reevaluate myself based on my own feelings and the input I receive from others. This reevaluation gives me a consistent means of understanding my improvement over time because of the baseline provided by my original evaluation. By developing an initial understanding of the areas I needed to work on to improve myself as a leader, I have been able to measure my progress toward my leadership goals. Think of it as your roadmap to personal improvement. I always use my evaluation graph and my resume as two points of reference to identify where I am on my career path. The resume is as important as the graph. It is a concrete representation of your actual experience and, done properly, can help you to understand those gaps you still need to address.

> By comparing the graph from your self-awareness exercise to your current resume, you can identify gaps in your experience and use those gaps to develop a self-improvement plan that coincides with your personal goals.

Be Prepared

In almost every speech I give around the country, I always ask the audience, "If you had that killer job offer today, the one you have always been waiting for, is your resume ready to present?" Most of the time when I ask this question, only a third of the audience members can raise their hands. Most people fail to understand that keeping your resume current is not about wanting to change jobs or looking to change jobs; it is really a way to create a dossier of your experiences. It is a method by which you can document your successes and identify weaknesses you can improve upon. Think of the items on your resume as guide posts on your personal path to success.

By comparing the graph from your self-awareness exercise to your current resume, you can identify gaps in your experience and use those gaps to develop a self-improvement plan that coincides with your personal goals. Use that plan as your professional development guideline. I used to refer to mine on a regular basis to make sure it was up to date and to help me set my personal development priorities based on my personal goals and the feedback I was getting from the marketplace. For example, at any time I might be working on presentation skills, collaboration skills, creative thinking, global experience, or relationship building. As part of my development plan, I create a checklist that parallels my resume. On it I list all the attributes necessary to becoming a leader so I can compare my achievements to the achievements I believe necessary to meet my leadership goals. Based on personal evaluation and feedback, I even prioritize the list based on my personal point of evolution as a leader. After completing an item on my checklist, I update my resume to reflect my accomplishment. This is my way of keeping abreast of market demands and ensuring my resume is current at all times. As I said earlier, you never know when the opportunity of a lifetime might be presented to you. Make sure you are ready.

Make Time for You and Live in the Moment

Part of being prepared for opportunity is being aware of it when it comes your way. We are often so caught up in the day-to-day that we miss opportunities. The most important ones are sometimes the most subtle. A call from a friend that you don't have time to respond to could be the next great opportunity. A meeting outside work that you didn't attend might have provided an opportunity to meet someone who could help you or to join a discussion that would have helped you resolve a problem you were dealing with. You need to adjust your priorities and pace to limit the number of opportunities that pass you by as much as possible. This is not easy to do; however, it is imperative that you balance your time and slow down to the speed of your surroundings.

In the book *Slowing Down to the Speed of Life*, Richard Carlson and Joseph Bailey write about learning how to live at the speed of life.[2] One of the passages that always comes to my mind involves a family sitting on a beach on a tropical island on a perfect day. Faced with this beautiful day, the family is discussing what to do the following day. They completely fail to experience the current moment for thoughts of what is next. This is a good example of what happens in corporate life today. We're always planning for the next question on the agenda. We never take the time to sit and enjoy the moment we are in now. Life is a short journey, and the older we get the more we realize that. Cherish the current moment; don't miss it by planning future moments.

I call it living in the moment. That book had a profound influence on me and since reading it I try to make every day unique and meaningful. I have found through the years that living in the moment makes me a better leader. It forces me to deal with events as they occur rather than letting them pile up or be ignored. There is a saying, "never put off to tomorrow what you can do today." Slowing down and living in the moment allows you to better address life's experiences in real time. One day I might learn how to delegate better, another I might learn how to manage my time better, but appreciating what is happening now rather than looking for what might happen tomorrow or the next day allows me to focus on my personal path. This type of mindfulness is essential to forming your leadership skills and becoming a trusted business partner. Failing to slow down to the speed of the day means things are overlooked, mistakes are made, and good decisions happen only by accident.

In today's world, we are constantly rushing to the next event. I have a friend who uses the expression "striving and not arriving." I think that really sums up the environment in corporate life today. We are all running toward something, and most of us don't even know what it is we are trying to catch. We need to be more diligent about living in the moment, managing our time, allocating our time for those things that are really important (including business concerns), but more importantly providing the time to focus on ourselves and the people around us and the relationships that we are building with our peers. Your relationships are a constant in your life, and they are the foundation of any leader's success.

Seek a Mentor

There is no replacement for experience, and corporate life is no exception. The funny thing about corporate life, however, is that most of the day-to-day activities haven't changed much through the years. It is still about people working with people, teams solving problems, decisions, communication, and an ability to work well with others. True mentorship can be a fast track to effective leadership by helping develop your skills in these essential areas. Seeking out more experienced people allows you to learn from their experiences before you make the same mistakes.

I have been mentoring executives for several years now, and it continues to amaze me that what is intuitive to me is often a brand-new insight to them. I sit back and watch as we work through day-to-day problems and laugh to myself because they are the same problems I have seen hundreds of times in my career. It reminds me of the time when my grandson was sitting at the kitchen table with me and after the meal I went to the cupboard to get a toothpick and as I sat at the table and started to use the toothpick, my grandson looked at me and asked, "Grandpa, what's that you have in your hand and what are you doing to yourself?" My immediate response was "It's a toothpick and I'm cleaning my teeth." Then I realized he had never seen one before and he didn't know what a toothpick was or what it was used for. It was obvious to me, but it was a new experience to him. This is what mentoring can do for you as you advance in your career. It gives you the ability to learn from the practical experiences of others so you don't make the same mistakes. It is so much easier learning from others than having to learn everything firsthand.

> Seeking out more experienced people allows you to learn from their experiences before you make the same mistakes.

The most important aspect of choosing a mentor is selecting the right person. An ideal mentor is someone who not only has extensive experience but shares a lot of values and personal traits with you. It doesn't work when you have two people with opposing values. Our experiences and the way we approach problems are important parts of our personality, and having someone with a similar personality makes it easier for you to learn from your mentor.

My first mentor was a local businessman in the New Hampshire town where I grew up. He came from a similar working-class background and was an active member in my church. He was a wonderful man who was very approachable. He always showed concern and interest whenever you came to him. He had been through World War II and suffered some lifelong injuries, but he didn't let that prevent him from striving for success. He built one of the largest businesses in my small town and was one of the most respected members of the community. I spent many days during the summer working for him and observing his behavior and interactions with others. We spent many hours talking about what it took to be successful, how important it was to be fair and honest with others, and how important it was to be honest with yourself. I still value the many life lessons he taught me, and I have passed them along to my children and clients. The most important thing he taught me was to always try to look at the good in others. It is easy to find fault with others, but it takes a strong person to find the good in people. This attitude provides an important tool for any leader because it is easier to face a challenge when you are thinking about the strengths of your team rather than their weaknesses.

My next mentor was a neighbor in New Jersey. He spent his entire career at a major financial firm, where he rose through the ranks to become its CEO. He taught me about the importance of personal relationships in building a successful career. He also emphasized that success requires a delicate balance between work, family, and health. If you dedicate too much attention to one, the others suffer. I still work to maintain that balance today. Indeed, balance in conjunction with working at the speed of the day is essential to becoming an effective leader today.

Are You in Balance?

Much of our lives are defined by priorities that are out of balance. We devote too much time to work, family, or health concerns and we fail to find that balance point where we can effectively focus on all three. Most of us dedicate too much effort to our work and not enough to the other two areas. Approaching your life and work without finding a successful balance can adversely affect both your professional and personal lives.

One summer when my son was in elementary school I attended one of his baseball games and noticed a man standing at the fence reading the *Wall Street Journal*. His son kept coming over and asking him to watch when he got in the game. The father felt compelled to continue reading his paper rather than watching the activities on the field. My heart went out to that boy and to his father. I could understand the anguish of the son trying to attract his father's attention and wishing to be successful in his father's eyes. I also felt bad for the father because he was so consumed by his job and by the business world that he couldn't take time to acknowledge what was really important. It is about family; it is about life experiences; it is about the speed of life that makes things relevant in today's world. I often think of that father standing at that fence as a reminder about the importance of balance.

As you start your journey up the corporate ladder, never forget the things that are important in life. Other people cannot provide you with all the answers, but you can benefit by sharing in their experiences. Some provide models for you to emulate; others may serve as examples of what to avoid. It gets back to your comfort zone: creating a balance between the advice of others and your own comfort level will make you successful.

What Motivates You?

What really motivates you? This may sound like a simple question, but the answer forms a key part of your self-evaluation. How you react to others and how you react as a leader are both tied to personal motivation. The means by which you accomplish things is based on your self-motivation. Understanding your motivations helps you achieve balance in your day-to-day life.

Throughout my career, I have always been motivated by a desire for change. I love to encounter change on a daily basis; every day I go into the office looking for something new. I have always said to myself, "Make every day unique; make every day different; find something about each day that can cause change or break routine." I look for change on a daily basis to this day because the older I get the more I recognize how few

31

days I have left and how important it is to make the most of each day. Others are motivated by a desire to avoid change. Discovering what truly motivates you allows you to adjust your behavior, organize your day, and adapt your work process to better reflect your motivation.

Competition is another big motivator for me. I have driven racecars for more than 20 years, and I thrive on the competition. It is not about winning at all costs; rather, it is about being at your best on a particular day. It is about making mistakes and learning from them. Mostly it is about the thrill of the chase. You don't have to be in the lead to feel the thrill of racing; there are many races within the race. Observers always focus on the leaders, but the best racing often takes place in the middle of the pack. Drivers have a saying that captures why being in the race is even more important than winning: "You never know how fast you can go if you never spin out." Unless you push yourself to achieve more than you have previously, you can never really know how good you can be. Many times during my racing career my son has pointed out to me that we will never improve unless we move up to the next level. Racing the same people, working the same problems, or always staying within your comfort zone never provides you an opportunity to improve. This is true in corporate life just as it is in racing. If you don't continually challenge yourself to be the best you can at everything you do it is not possible to discover what you might achieve and you will spend your life chasing the pack. Don't be afraid to increase your game, take on new challenges, or move into new areas you may not fully understand. Life is about risk, so be a risk taker and don't be afraid to take a chance. Life's journey isn't fixed, and there are no certain outcomes. You must be willing to break the mold, take an extra change, go the extra mile, and push yourself beyond what you think your limits are if you hope to lead.

Unless you push yourself to achieve more than you have previously, you can never really know how good you can be.

Do You Have Passion?

Another important thing for you to evaluate is your level of passion. Leadership, like life, is all about passion. When you talk to someone, you can always tell when the subject of conversation turns to something he or she feels passionate about. I know that when I talk about racing, a warm feeling of excitement comes over me. I can feel my conversation become more engaging. You can always recognize the passion in others. You see it in their eyes and in their body language. You hear it in their vocal inflections. A leader will try to find that passion in others, because accessing someone's passion makes that person more open and communicative. Building on that passion allows you to create rapport and a sense of camaraderie.

Your passion is an asset; everyone looks for passion in a leader. Few people will believe in you until they can hear passion in your voice. When you have a point to make, make it passionately. That is what makes people react, rather than just having a bland conversation. Passion isn't about controlling a conversation, having the loudest voice, or showing the most emotion—it is about a sincere effort to portray your ideas with conviction. If that doesn't convince your listener, it will at least lead to a careful consideration of your point.

Of course, passion can produce negative effects as well. We need to differentiate positive passions from those that create a negative response. Even children can tell whether we are passionate or angry. Passion is an emotion that people can relate to positively as long as you are positive in your passion. Don't be overly passionate or so expressive of your passion that you make people uncomfortable. Harnessing your passion means showing emotion in a controlled manner while still conveying to people the enthusiasm you have for the topic at hand. Just because you are passionate about a topic doesn't mean everyone else is. Learn to temper your passion to the current audience and context. Know when to be aggressive and when to be a little more laid back. When in doubt, tone it down—but never totally eliminate it.

Take direction from your audience. If people don't share your passion, draw them in and bring them along using shared experiences, common ideas, and similar interests. Help people use their own experiences and interests to build their passion for your idea. It is actually fun to watch people's opinions evolve as you motivate them. I always look for common ground first and then use it to guide the discussion. Everyone feels passionate about something, and finding common sources of passion is a great way to build a relationship.

> Harnessing your passion means showing emotion in a controlled manner while still conveying to people the enthusiasm you have for the topic at hand ... help people use their own experiences and interests to build their passion for your idea.

What Will I Be When I Grow Up?

The question your self-evaluation will answer is, "What will I be when I grow up?" I had a conversation with several friends around a table one night, and we talked about what we wanted to be when we were in our teenage or college years.

Interestingly, each of us had pursued a totally different profession. We debated if our personalities or our experiences led us into our careers.

I tend to believe that a combination of inner motivation, life's circumstances, and a little bit of luck brings us to our careers. When I was young, my greatest desire was to become an aviation engineer. I wanted to design jets—and fly them. Anything to do with airplanes interested me. What I ignored in my dreams of becoming an engineer was the extreme mathematical proficiency required to succeed in the field. Math was definitely not my strongest area in high school. As in most areas of my life, I was impatient with the details of mathematical concepts and formulas—I just wanted to get to the stage of designing airplanes without learning the basic skills required to design a plane successfully. That was another one of life's lessons: You have to create a strong foundation before you can place a building atop it.

I never quite made it to aviation school. Instead, I moved into the information technology field, which was called *data processing* then. In the Army, I volunteered for a test program that used computers to teach Morse code. I found that computers intrigued me, and I realized there was a great future in technology. My experiences in the Army helped me fully understand where I needed to be.

It is amazing how that passion lay dormant inside me, and it may have never come out had I not taken the chance opportunity provided by the Army. I wonder sometimes how many of us narrowly missed our calling in life because a random choice limited our exposure, or because the right opportunity never came along. I believe it is never too late to consider things we might have missed. You never know where the brass ring might come from. As I explained earlier, life is not a predefined journey: It is based on our day-to-day experiences. Each of us has an inert desire, and a capability based on our personality;

however, it never comes out until you are given the chance to exercise it.

> True leaders are successful because they seize these minor opportunities and create major successes from them.

Having grown up in Boston, of course I'm a New England Patriots fan. I remember the day Drew Bledsoe was injured and had to take a seat on the sidelines. A new young kid named Tom Brady came in to replace him. He lived in Bledsoe's shadow for several seasons, but it was now his time to shine. What makes him unique is that he made the most of that opportunity and became one of the best quarterbacks in NFL history. I've often wondered whether Tom Brady would have achieved such success if Drew Bledsoe had never been hurt. The positive side of me says that somewhere he would have performed whether it was in New England or another team; however, the other side of me says if he was never placed in the right position and given that opportunity he would never have succeeded. You can control a certain amount of your destiny in life. However, a lot of it is based on circumstance, situation, and luck. True leaders are successful because they seize these minor opportunities and create major successes from them. That transformation is what you should aim to achieve if you aspire to become one of tomorrow's leaders.

Notes

1. Donald J. Trump with Tony Schwartz, *The Art of The Deal* (New York: Random House, 1995).
2. Richard Carlson and Joseph Bailey, *Slowing Down to the Speed of Life: How to Create a More Peaceful, Simpler Life from the Inside Out* (New York: HarperCollins, 2009).

CHAPTER 3

Are You Ready to Make a Move?

C hanging jobs is like changing racecars. It is all about comfort, confidence, and security. When you are driving a racecar, you want to focus on the track and what is happening
around you. What you don't what to focus on is your car. Your
old car was molded to your body: The seat fitted perfectly,
the gearshift was in exactly the right place, the steering wheel
was the right length for your arms, so you never had to think
about the car. You knew every nuance, every sound, and how
to feel the car on the track. Driving a racecar is very different
from driving a car on the open road. In racing, it is all about
the feel of the car as it connects with the track and the feel
of your body inside the car. Changing cars has always been a
rather traumatic experience for me. You have to start all over
again. We spend endless hours making a new seat and molding
it to my body, adjusting the pedals, adjusting the steering wheel,
positioning the gearshift, and understanding the right height for
my body inside the car. You don't just jump in the new car
and go fast. It takes a lot of time building up to that level. You
first have to overcome the insecurity of leaving your old car behind. It is like leaving an old friend; you abandon your comfort
zone and the sense of security that arose from familiarity every
time you buckled yourself into your car. In a new car, everything is different and I'm starting all over to build a brand-new

relationship. Like racing, corporate life requires concentration, a strong relationship with your team, confidence, and a positive mental attitude.

Confidence and a positive mental attitude are imperative to success in most aspects of your life. Success driving a racecar is more about your mental fitness and awareness than anything else. You are battling your mind on every turn because your mind is saying that the car is incapable of performing the way it needs to, and the car is telling you "yes, I can." In order to be successful, you need to develop a comfort zone for yourself within the car. That is why it is so difficult when you change cars. You are giving up that comfort and security and starting all over again. Like switching racecars, before you make a change in the business world, you need to really consider the importance of the change and how it will affect you in the short and long terms.

If you don't properly understand and plan for changes, you may never fully recover should you make a bad decision. This is especially true in corporate life when moving from one company to another. Before considering a move, you need to go through a personal discovery process. Changing a job, just like changing a racecar, requires a certain amount of courage, faith, and belief in yourself. You need to take the time to understand your motivations for changing positions as well as the possible consequences of that decision. Having said that, I have changed jobs many times in my career and each new job has been better than the last. This wasn't luck; it was planning. It gets back to the self-evaluation discussed in Chapter 2. You really need to understand the environment and culture in which you are comfortable and your personal goals for success. These will change throughout the years as you move from position to position, but a careful evaluation will provide you the information you need to make the right decisions.

In many aspects of our lives, we naturally gravitate toward and settle into comfort zones. However, these zones can also foster personal limitations. The longer you remain in an organization, the harder it becomes to break out of that zone.

When I changed jobs for the first time, I felt very comfortable in the position I was leaving. I was well respected with several successes under my belt, and I enjoyed working with my colleagues. However, comfort can be deceiving. The longer you remain in a company, the more you develop a comfort zone. You learn the language, adapt to the culture, and understand what it takes to get things done. You also get lulled into a false sense of security by believing that your situation will never end and by equating comfort with optimum performance. We often fail to realize how much time it requires to gain an intimate knowledge of an organization. It can take many months or even years to gain the information and skills necessary to perform our jobs well and to develop our comfort zones. In many ways, job comfort is a good thing. It makes us feel better, of course, but it also enhances our performance and helps us appreciate and support the organization. On the other hand, comfort can lead to complacency. In many aspects of our lives, we naturally gravitate toward and settle into comfort zones. However, these zones can also foster personal limitations. The longer you remain in an organization, the harder it becomes to break out of that zone.

The most significant change in my career was moving from the job where I had the longest tenure. As I stated before, the longer you are with a company the deeper the relationships go, the more ingrained you are in that culture, and the more secure you feel. The impulse we all have as we contemplate a new position is to try to replicate where we already are. This is a normal human trait. You have had several years of success, you have developed strong relationships, you have built a successful team, but now it is time to move to the next opportunity. Our first instinct is to rely on our past successes and try to emulate them in our next position. However, you need to leave the past behind you as you move to the next opportunity. If you allow this impulse to revert back to your comfort zone to shape the start of your tenure at a new company you will never be able to take risks, learn new things, and break out. It is okay to use your past experiences as a reference point, but you need to actively move on with a positive attitude that allows you to build the right model for the new situation. I have seen many executives fail because they were unable to overcome this hurdle. No two companies are the same, and no two positions are the same, so each job requires a different model for success. You need to move forward with a clear mind and the courage to know you have the background and the experience to create the proper model to succeed in your new position.

Evaluate Yourself and the New Position

A crucial step in charting your next move is gaining a clear understanding of the new organization you are about to join. As we have discussed, we each have a unique comfort zone in which we feel secure. Changing jobs and moving into a new organization threatens that security. Before making any move, sit down and conduct a reevaluation of yourself and your current job situation. List the reasons you want to change positions along with your career objectives. What do you like about your current position? What things do you dislike and want to change? Remember: Taking a job just for the sake of change—or even for the sake of more money—may not help you advance toward your long-term goal.

I always tell people that, in many important ways, you could put Velcro on the back of your company's logo and move it from building to building as you change jobs. Not that each job doesn't offer a unique culture and present unique opportunities and challenges, but most of the personnel and operational concerns you deal with on a day-to-day basis are the same from company to company. We like to think we are all unique and that we are the only ones dealing with these issues; however, that is not true. The people-to-people issues and the basic core operating principles of corporations are the same no matter where you go. I say this because it is natural to feel the grass is greener on the other side of the yard. It is not in most cases; it is the same grass you are dealing with, but it is on the other side of the yard. The problems may be more or less intense than where you are, or they may be in different areas, but in the majority of cases there is a similarity in business functions, business operations, and organizational interactions. All too many times we convince ourselves we may be making the wrong move at the wrong time. I've gotten countless calls from executives saying they needed to make a change because they couldn't stand the situation they were in any longer. When I sit down and talk with them and listen to the real reasons they want a change, it usually comes down to one or two issues, such as a desire for a change in their reporting relationship, or dissatisfaction with a specific project that presents some difficulty they see as insurmountable.

Remember: Taking a job just for the sake of change—or even for the sake of more money—may not help you advance toward your long-term goal.

These are situations where people are running away rather than making a calculated move to the next best opportunity. It is important when you are evaluating a change that you make sure you are not just running away from something that will likely be present in the next opportunity as well. You need to know how to deal with changes in management, and you need to know how to deal with projects or initiatives that don't turn out as intended. If you can't find solutions to this type of fundamental problem in one job, you are unlikely to be any more successful at the next corporation. I've attended many events outside the company with my peers and discovered that most of us are dealing with the same types of problems. This was an eye-opener for me very early on in my career, and I am thankful because it has helped me in my decision process since then when I am ready to change jobs. This type of understanding is why it is important for you to meet people in similar roles at other companies, join industry organizations, and expand your network to provide a broader perspective on your current job. The more you do this, the better you will understand that you are not unique, your company is not unique, and the problems you are dealing with are not unique.

We have taken a long time discussing the fact that functional and operational problems tend to be the same from corporation to corporation. So why bother changing jobs? The major reason to make a change is to improve yourself; to find an environment that presents new challenges and experiences that will allow you to grow and reach the next level in your career. It is like racing with the same people all the time. You never really get any better because you are just racing with people at the same ability. What you need to do is break out and move up to the next level; improve yourself by taking on the challenges and developing the skills of the people at that level. So considering a change is something that is not to be taken lightly. You need to understand what is motivating you to make the change and ensure that what you are doing is going to advance your career rather than send it back or just provide a lateral movement.

Dealing with the Change

When you move to a new company, the particular details of the job make it feel like you have entered a whole new world. You encounter new jargon, a new culture, and a new set of team-mates. Everything lies well outside your usual zone of comfort. I remember how scared I felt on my first day at a new job. It reminded me of starting school, when you moved from the comfort of home and family into a frightening roomful of strangers, facing a teacher you didn't know and a culture from which you had no idea what to expect. When you change jobs, you are usually abandoning a position where you have performed well and where you have understood the expectations of successful performance and stepping into an alien environment.

Such changes are quite dramatic. Our desire to smoothly transition, gain acceptance, and succeed in the new venture places an emotional burden on us. You can't overestimate the effects of this burden. Rather, you must recognize its symptoms (insecurity, nervousness, and loss of self-confidence) and fully understand their impact upon you. Again, your personal self-evaluation can help you adjust your behavior and your thought processes in order to succeed in the new environment, but entirely ignoring these emotional symptoms will hinder your success.

Confronting your emotions requires complete self-honesty. You must focus on your inner being and not allow outside factors to influence you. Dealing with and overcoming uncomfortable situations require a clear understanding of your feelings. Gaining this understanding allows you to adjust your behavior and your approach to your work to achieve the success you desire. It is a very personal process that must be conducted on an individual basis; it is not something that you can discuss openly with others. Although a mentor can help, at the end of the day you must recognize the personal adjustments, both emotional and behavioral, that are required to succeed.

You must recognize your impact on others as you are integrating yourself into a new position. This is true of your new coworkers, but it is also important to consider the effects of the change on those who are closest to you, your family. There is the old saying that we only hurt the ones we love, and it rings true in changes in your career, particularly when the change involves relocating your family. Our natural tendency is to exhibit our frustrations, insecurities, and uneasiness with the ones we love. I am definitely not a believer that you can become two different people at work and at home. There is no such thing as a successful Jekyll and Hyde. You need to be yourself, operate in your comfort zone, and feel good about your actions. Any change comes with frustration and setbacks; make sure you don't bring all your emotions home with you to your family as you are going through these troubling times. As I said before, I'm not saying that you should leave everything in the office because you can't be two people. It is important, though, to clearly understand the sources of your stress and address them directly rather than bringing the stress home and inflicting it on those closest to you.

Moving to a new position is not a personal decision, it is a family decision. You need to understand you are not the only one feeling the stress of the change. Your family is feeling it as well. In many cases, it requires uprooting your family, selling a home, and moving to a whole new community and culture. I've done this several times in my career and each time we would move to a new area I would always tell my children it provided a unique opportunity to select a whole new set of friends. I can only imagine how stressful it was for them the first day of school in the new community where they didn't know anyone. So when you start feeling sorry for yourself after changing to a new position, just try to remember how the move has affected your family. It is not just about you: It is about the entire family. You need to share your concerns, you need to listen, and you need to work together as one team as you go through this integration process.

I remember a funny story from our first move after our children had grown and left home. We moved from the East Coast to the Midwest, just my wife, our dog, and me. We packed up all the household goods—including our cars—and my wife, the dog, and I jumped on a plane and flew to the new city. It was about three days later when our goods arrived and we began to unload them. One of the first things unloaded was my wife's car. It was a Dodge Caravan. They unloaded the car and opened the doors and we were checking it over when I looked up and there was our dog comfortably sleeping in the back seat. He had lost his world when we made the move, and that car became his security blanket. People suffer the same stresses with change, and we can have similar reactions when trying to deal with the stress. We need to understand that and develop coping mechanisms. I'm happy to say that after a few weeks the dog finally quieted down and began to accept his new surroundings. However, every time my wife would open the door to her car, the dog would jump in.

I once left a very secure job to start my own business. I believed the corporate world was holding me back and I wanted to see what new opportunities entrepreneurship presented. I didn't think through the consequences of that move. I acted based on emotion rather than common sense, and the result was that I put my family and myself in a very precarious position. This mistake cost me dearly, both emotionally and financially. Fortunately, I was able to get my old job back—a very rare occurrence. Because I didn't take the time to analyze my motivations for leaving the position, my family and I suffered the negative consequences of my hasty decision.

Never act only on emotions; consider your situation rationally and holistically before you take the plunge. I was very lucky. Few people get the luxury of returning to their old jobs. I'm not trying to scare you, but I want you to understand that you cannot make important, life-changing decisions quickly. Ask a lot of questions. Seek advice from your friends. Talk to your family. And most importantly, conduct a careful self-evaluation before you make the move.

> Never act only on emotions; consider your situation rationally and holistically before you take the plunge.

Do Your Homework

It is also very important to fully research any company to which you plan to move. Talk to as many people as you can, read all the available literature, and make sure that you gain an in-depth knowledge through your interview process. The interview is a critical step in achieving your goal, but don't enter an interview with the sole intention of selling yourself to a company. It should be a mutual experience of discovery. Make sure you examine the company as carefully as it examines you. If, after an initial interview, there is mutual interest to move to the next step, take the time to interview the key leaders in the corporation. Don't request only that they interview you—interview them as well. This two-way interaction accomplishes a lot. It allows you to learn about the corporation, it allows the corporation to learn about you, and it helps you begin to develop personal relationships.

If, after an initial interview, there is mutual interest to move to the next step, take the time to interview the key leaders in the corporation. Don't request only that they interview you—interview them as well.

One thing I like to do when I am evaluating a new company and considering a change is to gain an understanding of the company's current point of evolution. What I mean by that is determining whether the company is about to embark on a long period of sustained growth, whether it has reached a level of maturity where it is stable and has a rather limited growth curve, or whether it is at the end of a growth curve. This also holds true for the industry in which the company works. You need to make sure the company and its point of evolution align with your personal expectations. Later in our careers, some of us may well accept a position with a company that is at the end of its growth curve because we don't have a long-term requirement for aggressive growth and the opportunity, the compensation, the team, or the culture fit with our expectations. If you are younger and looking to rapidly advance your career, this type of situation would not be a good fit. You would be much better served in a company that is at the beginning of its growth curve and looking to have a long sustained period of growth. Many of us never take the time to understand the point of evolution as we investigate our next opportunity. Taking this step is extremely critical as you may find that you have made the wrong decision and it is too late to do anything about it as you are now committed. Match the opportunity to your individual need and make sure the situation matches your current career requirements. In some cases you might want to take a position in a company that is not growing just to achieve a particular title. I was able to get my first CIO position with a company that was in chapter 11. We all know the first appointment to a new role is the most difficult, so you might want to take a chance to break through. In my case, we came out of bankruptcy and I was able to leverage the position to get a better one.

At this point in your investigation, you should also develop an understanding of your prospective employer's expectations for your specific area if you decide to move to the company. For example, if you are taking over a technology group within the company, learn from the top-level executives how they view technology, how important it is to the success of the company, and what they see as the major projects on the horizon as part of the company's technology strategy. This will help you begin to understand whether the position is a good fit for you at the current stage of your career. Too many times we don't take the initiative to really understand the perceptions and culture of the new organization we are about to join. I'm not saying the organization you are about to take over must be totally respected by the corporation; otherwise, they wouldn't be looking for a leadership change. What I am saying is that you should find out if the other leaders are willing to provide you with the support necessary to succeed. Do they recognize the potential value of your organization and what it can contribute to the overall success of the corporation?

> You should find out if the other leaders are willing to provide you with the support necessary to succeed.

Many people feel it is extremely important to their success that they report to the most senior executive at the corporation. I know many people who have passed on tremendous opportunities because they would have reported to the chief finance officer (CFO) or the chief operations officer (COO) as opposed to the chief executive officer (CEO). I would suggest that you don't let that impede your decision to move to a new company.

All too many times I have observed my peers accepting a job that reported to the CEO only to find that he or she had very little interest in their area. It became very hard for them to find a champion for their cause as the rest of the leadership team also understood that the CEO did not find their specific area of strategic importance. This can put you in a very dangerous situation. The better alternative is to find the executive with the most passion for your organization and what he or she can achieve for the corporation. You would be far better served to report initially to that person and partner with him or her and use that partnership to gain immediate success and the respect of the rest of the leadership team. After you have done that, it opens the door for you to change your reporting relationship at a later time. Moving up to reporting to the CEO after a series of successes and a partnership with one of the other major executives will give you credibility, a proven track record, and a strong relationship with the rest of the team, which will allow you to overcome any prejudices the CEO may have about your organization. So don't get hung up on whom you report to when considering a move to your next position; what you really need to know is who in that organization has the most passion for what you want to achieve.

> So don't get hung up on whom you report to when considering a move to your next position; what you really need to know is who in that organization has the most passion for what you want to achieve.

The Integration Process

When you change positions, you undergo a very unsettling process as you gradually become integrated into the new organization. IT groups constantly inflict change upon organizations, but they are usually reluctant to accept change within themselves. Changing an organization is always a daunting task, but trying to change yourself presents a far greater challenge. As stated earlier in this chapter, you need to put your prior position behind you and move on to this new challenge unburdened by prejudices or preferences developed at your previous position.

My biggest mistake when entering a new position was to compare everything in the new organization to something from the organization I just left. Now, when I coach other IT executives, I tell them to learn from past positions, but never try to re-create them. Every company's situation is different, and you can always apply your experiences without insisting on recreating your past environments. Through the years I've found that, from an IT perspective, managing from organization to organization is basically the same. The differences lie in company cultures and the methods of getting things done.

During the integration process, it is imperative to remain patient. I remember how uneasy I felt at a new job and the personal stress my transition caused. To avoid this, you must allow yourself a sufficient period to become integrated into the new corporation. There is no fixed timeframe for completing this process. Assimilation into some companies is easier than into others, depending on organizational complexity, but in all cases you can only integrate effectively if you temper your emotions and internal stresses.

I remember the first few times I drove a racecar. I was frightened and unable to comprehend all the things that were occurring around me. Between trying to watch what was going on inside and outside the car, and trying to manage my own emotions, I felt totally out of control. Thank heavens I had a great instructor who could guide me through the process. He made me focus on one or two things at a time, then gradually develop other skills. First, I became comfortable inside the car—making sure that the pedals and steering wheel were in the right positions, that the gauges could be seen clearly, and that the gearshift was within reach. When you can relax in the cockpit while sitting in the pits, it is time to drive the track slowly, learning the turns and breakpoints and locating the flagging stations. The next step is to learn to glance at and understand your gauges while driving. As you practice, you build your speed and become comfortable and confident in the car. You push yourself and the car more with each session, learning your limits and the nuances of the track and gaining the information you need to effectively compete. Eventually, it all becomes second nature.

As in racing, corporate life requires a gradual development process to build your confidence and skills so you can excel at the highest possible level. It's done through a series of small steps, each building on the next and each designed to increase your awareness, capability, and knowledge. Integrating yourself into a new organization is like getting comfortable in a racecar. You don't want to rush off in such a hurry that you overlook key steps along the way. Rather, master each step individually before moving on to the next. Then you will be successful.

Each and every time I moved to a new organization, I would reach a point when I felt I would never comprehend everything necessary to be recognized as a positive contributor. Then all of a sudden a light bulb would go off and everything became clear. It's amazing how taking your time, listening, and learning prepares you so all of the pieces come together suddenly in your mind. It has happened to me time and again. Even so, I still tend to suffer from that initial insecurity when I move into a new situation. You need to believe in yourself and you need to believe in the process. You need the confidence that, given the right opportunity, you will become comfortable in your new position and begin to build the trusting relationship that is so important for you to become a business partner with the leaders in the company. Everyone around you will respect you more if you move into a new position and demonstrate that you are humble, communicative, and willing to listen to those around you. People instinctively want to help those who humble themselves. It is not a sign of weakness to move into a new situation and a new environment and admit to your peers that you are a bit uncomfortable and that you would welcome their support and assistance so you can gain the understanding of your organization necessary for you to work effectively with them.

Moving to a new company can be like moving to a new country where the culture and language are unfamiliar. Just as attempting to speak the local language when you are in a foreign country can lead residents to bend over backward to help you communicate, being honest with your new peers and demonstrating your willingness to learn their language and culture breaks down a major barrier, helps them relate to you, and encourages them to help you integrate yourself into the company. This is not to say there won't be those who might view you as a threat or have such an ego they don't feel it necessary to coach you or teach you, but the majority of those with whom you will be interacting will welcome the opportunity to reach out to you if you first reach out to them.

> Everyone around you will respect you more if you move into a new position and demonstrate that you are humble, communicative, and willing to listen to those around you.

Building the Foundation of Trust

The integration process is a critical step in helping you build a foundation for a set of trusted relationships. The way you behave during the integration process is of critical importance. As stated earlier, it is so important to reach out and be communicative, approachable, and humble as you deal with people in your new environment. This could also be said of your current environment for those of you who have never changed jobs or are looking to move to the next level with your current company. It is all about how you approach people with whom you are seeking to build relationships or from whom you are seeking information.

We all know trust is something that takes time to build; however, first impressions are critically important in building long-standing trusting relationships. Most people form an opinion of you based on your initial introduction, so it is important during that introductory process to conduct yourself in the collaborative humble manner I've discussed. It is much easier to integrate in a new position if people form a favorable opinion of you based on your initial interactions than it is if you have to change people's opinions at a later date. One of the best ways to initiate this process is to be a good listener and to ask a lot of questions. The more questions you ask of others, the more comfortable they become with you and, subconsciously, the more likely they are to seek out a relationship with you. What you really are doing is asking your new peers to open themselves up to you so you can learn from them how you should form a relationship with them. Most people are flattered when someone is willing to take the time to first listen to them before beginning to talk about himself or herself.

> It is much easier to integrate in a new position if people form a favorable opinion of you based on your initial interactions than it is if you have to change people's opinions at a later date.

When I'm introduced to someone for the first time and that person immediately breaks into a conversation about his or her personal experiences and background, I find myself turned off. I would much rather people introduce themselves and then immediately start asking questions of me. A benefit of encouraging your new peers to talk about themselves is that while you are asking questions and people are responding, you are able to adapt your responses to their comfort zone. The questions give you intelligence about your peers as individuals: what makes them tick, how they think, and how they may react to you and to different situations. Observing this behavior gives you the time to mold your responses in a manner that is consistent with the characteristics of the person to whom you are speaking. There is no one-size-fits-all approach to building rapport, and it is crucial to take the time to understand as much of the inner being of the person with whom we are communicating as possible as we begin to build this relationship.

The best place for you to start practicing this type of communication is in settings with which you are familiar. It could be a cocktail party with friends, a family function for a holiday, or a professional event that you always attend. I always found these to be the best environments to begin to mold my approach to new people. It is much easier to approach someone with whom you have a somewhat familiar relationship than to approach a perfect stranger. It is interesting when you do this how the interaction with those you are talking to changes. You see a change in their behavior and their demeanor and the way they address you, even though you thought you knew these people for a long time and have an intimate knowledge of them. It is the subtle differences in the way you interact with them that cause them to change their behavior. What you are doing here is really getting yourself closer to someone else's comfort zone. You are accommodating yourself to another person rather than asking him or her to accommodate to you. I can remember through the years my wife and I always found it to be much more work being a friend than we ever thought. Being a friend means going the extra distance yourself, taking the initiative yourself, being the one to contact your friends regularly and invite them to your home, and communicating with them on a regular basis. When first starting out, you feel it is unfair that you have to be the one to initiate contact in most cases; however, after a while it becomes second nature to you. You will find that the more you reach out over time, the more the people to whom you reach out will begin to reciprocate. You achieve greater balance in your relationships the longer you build them.

> You will find that the more you reach out over time, the more the people to whom you reach out will begin to reciprocate.

This is true in the corporate environment as well. You need to be the one driving the relationship, communicating regularly, and organizing your interactions. It's up to you, even though you are the new kid on the block, to aggressively pursue new relationships with your peers. The people at the new corporation already have relationships with each other and with other members of the corporation's teams. You are the one responsible for integrating yourself into their team rather than vice versa. It is not easy trying to be the one to lead the development of relationships, but over time you get more and more comfortable with it. As mentioned earlier, the best way to practice is on those you know and who are closest to you. Developing that skill with those in your comfort zone will make it easier for you when you are required to do it in a professional setting.

The more proficient you become in these skills, the easier it will be for you to become a trusted member of a new business team. The process can be personally draining for those of us who are uncomfortable in these situations; however, the rewards far outweigh the pressures. Don't hold back. Be the person everyone wants to communicate with, lead the conversation, lead the relationship building, take the offense when building relationships and you will find that over time you'll build stronger, better, and longer lasting connections with those around you.

CHAPTER 4

Developing Your Leadership Style

Have you ever attended a party and noticed that everyone seemed to be listening to one or two people in the room? I've seen this phenomenon countless times and have tried to identify the characteristic that causes me to stop and pay attention to these individuals. Why do they become the center of the discussion? What draws others to them? To be blunt, these people are interesting. Their topics of discussion are neither generic nor boring. Their delivery—both verbal expression and body language—draws us in and appeals to our senses. They project an approachable demeanor that engages the listener and fosters a sense of personal contact. But is it natural charisma that governs their social behavior? I believe this: They have successfully developed their leadership style.

During the past few years, I have toured the country with the heads of leading search firms conducting panel discussions on leadership and the qualities companies look for in potential leaders. I've learned from these experiences that there is no strict definition of leadership. They all say that they are looking for strong leaders, but they seem to describe the characteristics of a strong leader differently. Many people form their perception of a strong leader based on personal experiences. In many ways, people are looking for someone who stands apart from the crowd. I have spent many years observing group behavior. No matter what size the group, there is one person who always emerges as the leader. The common trait these leaders seem to share is an ability to grasp the subject of the discussion and articulate it in a way everyone understands. They are more physically expressive, yet not overbearing. They have a balanced delivery. They display a comfortable yet believable persona and are collaborative and approachable. They have a unique ability to absorb the topics of discussion and synthesize them into easily understood actions. It is those subtle traits that make them stand out. They are good listeners and ask many questions. They also are not afraid to admit what they do not know. Good leaders are able to consistently build productive and efficient organizations by selecting the best talent.

> The common trait these leaders seem to share is an ability to grasp the subject of the discussion and articulate it in a way everyone understands.

Leadership is an intangible; strong leaders may share certain characteristics and personality traits, but leadership is acquired through life experiences, both inside and outside the workplace. One of the reasons leadership is so difficult to define is that it is expressed in so many settings. Whether we realize it or not, we have opportunities to exhibit leadership every day as parents, in our communities, and in our social and recreational activities. Some leadership talents are acquired based on experience; however, many are the result of our intrinsic characteristics and the environment in which we were raised. Childhood experiences have a tremendous impact on our leadership skills. There was only one class president and a limited number of other officers. Think about them and what you think made them able to aspire to those offices.

Building strong personal relationships is a key to success as a leader. People work best with people they like, and a good leader commands respect through personal interactions. This is true even in our personal lives. Think about the people you admire and enjoy being around. As you consider their traits and behaviors, you'll begin to recognize certain qualities that make you want to associate with and follow them. After you have observed this behavior in others, compare it to your own comfort zone. Note any specific traits or actions you might adopt comfortably. I'm not suggesting you model yourself on an individual; I'm suggesting you identify the behaviors of people you feel are good leaders and decide if any of them might work for you.

Leadership is always based on an individual style. It is a combination of personal strengths, learned behaviors, and individual comfort zones. You cannot lead effectively when you're operating outside your personal comfort zones. I tend to use levity in my interactions because a lighthearted tone helps make a discussion more comfortable for me and, I think, more comfortable for the people with whom I'm dealing. People tend to react more positively to a lighthearted tone than they do to a serious one. Of course, I often encounter situations that require me to adopt a serious tone, but in general, maintaining a cordial, jovial atmosphere has worked much better for me than have my attempts at trying to present myself as a dictatorial leader.

> Leadership is always based on an individual style. It is a combination of personal strengths, learned behaviors, and individual comfort zones.

Cast Your Own Shadow

Take the time to define and develop your specific style. How do you want to be perceived? How do you want to relate to others? Using your personality, your experiences, and the behaviors you have observed in others, create your own *shadow*. I use that term a lot. The best leaders have the ability to create their own shadow. Don't develop a persona that you think others will like; combine your experiences and your inner self to create a unique personal style. To succeed as a leader, you must be comfortable with yourself and with the shadow you cast.

> To succeed as a leader, you must be comfortable with yourself and with the shadow you cast.

We all need to cast our own shadow. Don't follow the crowd; create your own way in the world. That is not to say you always have to be different, but, you can't be afraid to strike out from the crowd. Believe in your convictions and most importantly, believe in yourself. Have the confidence to try something different. I always tell my people the ones who never make mistakes don't ever accomplish much. We need to challenge ourselves and look for that creative idea or new opportunity. In racing they have a saying, "You never know how fast you can go if you never spin out." Staying in line and following the crowd will never get you to the front of the pack.

I'm not saying there are no risks in taking a new path or interjecting a new idea, but I believe you will gain much more respect if you are willing to take a chance rather than always conforming. Leadership is a confidence game. It is all about risk and reward. Do your homework and research and then don't be afraid to take a chance. There is a balance between calculated risk and being reckless. When I am ready to attempt a pass in racing, I have followed the car in front of me for a couple of laps and I already know where I am faster. So I have done my homework and now it is time to execute. You can do the same in the business environment.

Leadership is an acquired skill gradually developed over the course of a personal journey. The principles that shape your leadership style will remain stable throughout your career; but you'll make subtle changes in how you act on those principles based on the experiences, successes, and failures you encounter. A smart leader never compromises these principles—and learns to hone his or her skills and image over time.

Many leaders make the mistake of adopting multiple styles: one for inside the corporation, another for outside the corporation. While this model might have worked many years ago, societal changes over the last several decades have made it difficult to operate effectively in a split-personality mode. Effective leadership is a consistent pattern of behaviors that governs the way we react to others every day in every situation, not something we can compartmentalize or turn off and on. We need to have one persona and one face in order to be successful. It is not about acting, but rather, about our core being. It is all about our interactions with others no matter the situation. When you try to be two different people, you usually are ineffective because you are perceived as inconsistent or flighty. We can't split our behavior. Take the time to develop your core leadership style and practice it in every situation. Being consistent and true to your core will help you build strong and trusted relationships. Leadership is about relationships—with a next-door neighbor, a subordinate, or your boss—and effectively connecting to others. There is no distinction between being effective inside your corporation and being effective outside your corporation. It is all about people and personalities, about building relationships and gaining the respect of others. We need to be ourselves wherever we go. People only associate with people they like and feel comfortable with.

Being consistent and true to your core will help you build strong and trusted relationships.

As you look back over your career, consider how you reacted to different managers and managerial styles. Don't ever forget where you came from, and use your experiences moving up the organization to better understand how you should behave as a leader. Remember the good and bad traits of leaders you have worked with and how you responded to their actions. It is safe to say that your reactions to the way these leaders treated you are consistent with the way others would feel if treated the same way. Let your experiences form the foundation of your leadership style as you mold yourself into the leader you always wanted to follow. Learn from the strengths and weaknesses of others. Combine that experience into a comfortable style that works for you. Always test yourself and ask for honest feedback from others. Never stop trying to improve.

Being a good leader is like being a good parent. We should strive to be consistent, fair, and trustworthy. Consistency means that what is wrong today will still be wrong tomorrow. It also means that we need to be consistent in our behavior. When we have a bad day, we cannot allow our moods to influence others in our organization. People interpret changes in behavior as a reflection of your feelings about them. That is why it is so important to remain consistent. If you address people consistently day after day, they become comfortable with you. If you change your behavior, they immediately suspect that something is wrong and build a defensive wall that is detrimental to your long-term relationship. You need not be happy and jolly all the time, but major changes in your behavior can have a direct impact on your subordinates as well as on your peers.

As a manager, I tend to wander a lot. I like to walk the halls, meet with my people, and engage them in conversation. This style works for me. During my wanderings, I often sit in cubicles with staff members and reminisce. For example, I would talk about how it felt to see the program I wrote actually run in production or how excited I felt when I was able to fix a major system problem. Such things now seem silly because I have gained more experience and have more meaningful ways to evaluate my success, but at the time they were serious topics of conversation between me and my peers. Taking the time to sit down and reminisce and joke with your team members can really help you establish a bond with them. It shows them that you have been there, and that you understand their needs and concerns. It helps them gain a new level of understanding and respect toward you. It is all about remembering the way you once felt, and never forgetting those things that motivated and discouraged you. It is a way to be the leader that you always wanted to work for, to cast your own shadow.

Consult a Mentor

As discussed in Chapter 2, while you mold your leadership skills, consult a mentor—someone you trust or, more importantly, someone who has a proven track record of success. Learning from the experiences of others increases the odds of achieving success yourself. An effective mentor can greatly accelerate your transition to becoming a leader. Some might say that a mentor is unnecessary, but I have found that I learned much about my own leadership style by collaborating with others. While there is no replacement for real-world experience, a mentor who has been there before can provide enormous help. A mentor is also a confidant with whom you can share ideas and concerns and test new theories and new behaviors.

Choosing the right mentor is a difficult decision and one you cannot take lightly. As you begin your selection process, try to find someone who shares your core principles and personality traits, not someone who is totally divergent from your outlook and behavior. You're looking for someone who can recognize your principles and help you mold your actions into an effective means of meeting those ideals. Someone with similar personality traits will bring a higher level of empathy, thereby increasing your chances of success. Make a list of the characteristics you feel offer you the best advantage in your transition to becoming an effective leader. This list can help you think about your core principles and become the basis of your selection criteria for a mentor.

A mentor need not share a similar job function with you. What you really want is someone with similar principles who has achieved success over a long period and developed a reputation as an effective leader. My first mentor was a neighbor in New Jersey. The CEO of a major corporation in New York City, he had worked his way up from the mailroom to the top. He was well respected in the community, well thought of by his peers, and recognized in the industry as a strong leader. I chose him because we shared many personality traits. He was a strong family man, religious, community oriented, and very much concerned with being fair and honest with his people. He was not self-indulgent, but rather, he took pride in the successes of people he led. He was more of a quiet leader than an outspoken one. He was the type of leader I wanted to become, and he was a person for whom I would have wanted to work as I was ascending the corporate ladder. His values, his personality, and his goals seemed quite consistent with mine.

In my racing career, my mentor was a much better instructor of drivers than he was a driver. He'd spent relatively little time driving a car himself, but he had an uncanny ability to instruct drivers at all levels, from entry-level racers to some of the most widely recognized professionals in the world. What made him an effective teacher was that he could apply a broad range of experiences to any situation I might encounter. Very little occurred on the track that he hadn't seen before. What made him an effective mentor was that we shared similar personalities and a similar approach to the sport.

His style was not to dwell upon your weaknesses, but to commend your strengths and to work with you on improving your skills. He employed a suggestive method rather than a dictatorial one, and he'd apply key phrases that still come to mind whenever I'm in my racecar. For example, he'd say, "You're coasting." He meant when you approach a corner at speed, you should be off the gas and on the brake. If not, you're coasting and slowing down the car too much. He would constantly remind me to be either on the gas or on the brake, but never in between. Another phrase, "Slow in, fast out," meant that as you enter a corner, you want to gain control of the car at the apex of the turn so that you can exit the corner at a much higher speed. Drivers learning the race craft always feel they have to enter the corner at a high rate of speed. This actually slows down their exit and their overall ability to keep pace. That is the kind of coaching you want: specific advice and reactions that you can apply to your day-to-day life.

Mentorship delivers a positive impact on your leadership style by making you more of a collaborator than a person who issues mandates. In many cases, we already know the answers to the questions we might ask a mentor, but sometimes it is good to gain reassurance that you're making the right decision. The most successful leaders I know regularly consult with others before making decisions. In today's rapidly changing world, going it alone is increasingly difficult, which makes it even more imperative to have a trusted source you can lean on. A mentor can help you navigate figurative mine fields based on his or her personal experiences. There is no replacement for experience. The smartest leaders I know have a mentor. They are successful because they have learned to fill their gaps in experience and understanding. They know what they don't know and seek guidance in those areas.

> The smartest leaders I know have a mentor. They are successful because they have learned to fill their gaps in experience and understanding. They know what they don't know and seek guidance in those areas.

I am currently mentoring five senior executives. Three are new to their current positions and the other two have been at the same company for an extended period of time. Each one of them is an individual with a unique personality as well as a unique background of experiences. The common theme for all of them, though, is that they know they have to make some adjustments in order to move on to the next level in their careers. This is something that is fairly unique to those who seek mentors as they have realized they need to seek outside help in order to grow their personal career. Just like the person at home who tries to fix everything himself, most of us try to go it alone only to find that the journey would have been much easier had we sought advice from an outside professional. I can't remember how many times I've tried to fix the kitchen sink only to have it continue to leak. In frustration I finally hire a plumber and the problem is immediately solved. This is how most successful people are able to continue the journey to the top of the organization; they have learned they can no longer go it alone and they need the help of others in order to fill those gaps in their own experiences and knowledge.

Leaders Succeed from the Bottom Up, Not the Top Down

The other important lesson most of the strong leaders that I know have learned is that leadership is built from below rather than from above. I can remember one specific time in my career when I was working for an extremely challenging company. We were in a period of rapid growth, with an ever-changing management team. Being early on in my career in leadership, I immediately assessed the situation and felt it was important for me to build a strong relationship with the CEO. At the time I reported to the CFO, so I had to do this in a way that did not seem threatening to him. I was able to initiate a lot of projects that were directly supportive of the CEO's efforts and thus was able to build a very good personal relationship with him. The mistake I made was that I didn't build strong enough relationships with those within my organization. They felt I was exerting all of my attention at the management level and not giving them the guidance and support they needed to be successful. In a situation like that, it doesn't take long before people start speaking with others outside your organization as well, and if you do not act on it quickly it can get well out of hand. It is easy to lose the confidence of the team and it is extremely hard to regain it. This is also true of the perceptions that can be created outside the organization. Perception is reality, and you need to be aware of the gravity of this type of situation. Give you team the guidance and leadership they are looking for and you will clearly display your worth as a leader.

I was fortunate that one of my direct reports was not afraid to speak up. She came to me and expressed her concerns that I was ignoring my organization while building relationships at the top. I would have regular staff meetings and meet with my direct reports on a regular basis. However, these meetings were mostly superficial and didn't really dig into the details of what was going on. In addition, I didn't spend enough time building personal relationships with my direct reports and listening to their concerns about the issues that were important to them. I was viewed as more of an opportunist than a leader. This type of behavior almost cost me my position at that job. Had it not been for the one direct report who was bold enough to come forward and make me aware of the situation, I probably would have. I immediately took steps to build a better relationship with those who reported to me in my department and as many of the other members of my department as I could. I would allocate a certain amount of time each day to just stop by and chat with them about work and about their personal concerns and interests. I also learned to listen more to their concerns about the issues they were dealing with and the concerns of their organization. It didn't take long before I was able to change the perception of my team. I maintained my strong working relationship with the CEO, but I balanced it with the relationships I was building within my own organization. Having created this balance provided me the opportunity to display leadership at both levels rather than just at one. It is imperative as you move up the leadership ladder to remember that the keys to success are held by those at your level or below rather than those on the level above.

> It is imperative as you move up the leadership ladder to remember that the keys to success are held by those at your level or below rather than those on the level above.

Since I had that experience, I've observed many others in similar situations. In one particular case, this person was able to build an extremely strong relationship with the CEO. They became strong personal friends and spent a lot of time together. However, this relationship was causing a lot of dissension among the ranks of his peers. It wasn't long before one of them was able to identify a weakness in his organization and expose it to the rest of the leadership team. I watched this unfold and as it became more apparent this was going to become a major issue, the CEO began to distance himself from this individual. It wasn't too long before he was nearly alone in the organization without support from above or below. Needless to say, it was a very short period of time before he was replaced. The biggest lesson learned here is you will always be safer and more secure in building strong relationships at and below your level than building strong relationships above that level.

I have also witnessed leaders who have been complacent in giving direction to their fellow team members. This results in a lack of confidence by the rest of the team. Once your team loses confidence in you, it becomes almost impossible for you to succeed. This doesn't happen in a day, a week, or a month; it takes time. However, left unaddressed it can destroy you as a leader. Once your team lacks confidence in your leadership they can become passively submissive. They will go through the motions to do their jobs and nothing more. They will no longer be the ones to identify sources of potential concern, instead saying nothing. This complacency is easily recognized by those outside of your organization, especially within the human resources group. Once that cancer starts to grow, the leader is usually doomed. The best way to avoid this type of problem is to be a team player, involve your team in decisions, and show your total support for them. This is the only way you can effectively become a trusted business partner.

As a leader, I always make time to understand the lives of as many of my team members as possible. Every one of them has a unique combination of families, challenges, and opportunities, and understanding this not only helps build strong relationships but helps me understand experiences and interests each member brings to the team. I try to spend personal time with as many team members as possible. Of course, in an organization of 2,000 people, you will never be able to spend the time you might like to with each person, but even if you can make the effort in smaller groups it is well received by all. When members of my team or their family have health problems or other challenges, I always make sure I take the time to sit with them and let them know that I understand their challenge and will work with them in any way I can to help. I also send cards and flowers when appropriate. These little touch points are important in becoming a trusted leader. It doesn't take much time out of every day to reach out to those individuals who are in need and let them know you care, and let them know you're there for them.

I always challenge my staff by asking, "If I could make all the right decisions, why would I need you?" I always consult with them, entrust them, and empower them, not only so they can grow as individuals, but also so they can properly assist me when critical decisions are required. I call this approach "managing by guardrails." I establish a set of parameters for each staff member—guardrails for them to operate within. As long as people remain within their guardrails, I leave them alone and empower them to make their own tactical decisions. This helps me build a tremendous amount of trust and loyalty with my staff. More importantly, it builds their experience and expertise, which lets me delegate more and more of the decision-making to trusted, competent individuals. As a result, I can devote more of my attention to larger strategic decisions. It also affords me the opportunity to interact more frequently with my leadership peers within the organization. A former boss once made a profound statement that still stays with me: He said that a good leader is one who can leave for a month and not be missed. This reinforces the management premise of delegating and building trust within your staff. I've always offered my staff opportunities to let me trust them, too. I will entrust them with small decisions and watch their responses. Then I increase the complexity and sensitivity of the issues and again monitor the results. Over time you gain a clear indication of individual capabilities and trustworthiness. Trust in your team is of paramount importance to your individual success. You cannot lead effectively if you do not have team members you can trust implicitly.

A former boss once made a profound statement that still stays with me: He said that a good leader is one who can leave for a month and not be missed. This reinforces the management premise of delegating and building trust within your staff.

The pace of change will not slow down; it will continue to accelerate. Today's seemingly impossible deadlines will only become tighter. As effective leaders, we must create a culture and an environment that gives us the capability of responding to tomorrow's challenges while mitigating today's risks. This requires a collaborative leadership style in which you consult with others and delegate to skilled team members.

Building a Strong Team

In additional to the overall success of the organization, a leader is judged by the quality and success of the individuals working under his or her supervision. A successful leader has a proven track record of developing strong, efficient organizations. This process starts with the leadership team. To be effective, you need to build a team that can not only work effectively, but can also broaden your own expertise. My friends in the major search firms focus on a critical metric when evaluating candidates for leadership positions: the careers of the staff they have developed over the years and the success of their former staff members who have moved on to leadership positions. Strong leaders staff their organizations with people who fill the gaps in their specific areas of expertise and experience. A weak leader often feels threatened by such individuals and fills staff positions with people of lesser ability. Don't be afraid to bring people who are better and smarter than you into every level of your organization. Not only will they help you improve as a leader, they will help you achieve the overall success that you are seeking.

> Don't be afraid to bring people who are better and smarter than you into every level of your organization.

Remember: A good leader can go away for a month and not be missed. The only way to accomplish this is by assembling a strong staff. The best place to start is to return to your self-evaluation. Review the areas in which you're strong and the areas that can use improvement. Next, consider your experience and compare it to the job at hand to understand what you're lacking and what a potential staff member might bring. Finally, consider your individual character strengths and weaknesses, and then seek individuals who possess the characteristics that you still need to develop. Such people will help enhance your overall performance. This inventory will give you a clear understanding of the personality traits, characteristics, and experiences that you're looking for in potential staff members. You'll be able to give any recruiters or search firms a clear set of instructions for identifying prospects, and you'll have definite guidelines to follow when interviewing candidates.

The final consideration when building your staff is to define the culture you want to develop within your organization. I've discussed the need to understand your company's culture; you also need to understand the separate team culture you'd like to build as a leader. Much of this will depend on the overriding culture of your corporation, on the point of evolution that your corporation has reached, and on the industry in which you operate. A company in an industry that is experiencing high growth and high challenges will require a completely different culture than one in a more traditional industry with more limited growth. The personalities of the individuals involved in either of these cultures may differ dramatically, and you will need to take that into account while building your staff. In order to create a cohesive organization in which people work well together and understand their objectives, you need a strong underlying culture. Overlooking this aspect of staff development can be detrimental to an organization's long-term success.

> The final consideration when building your staff is to define the culture you want to develop within your organization.

When interviewing candidates, I always ask, "What do you expect of me as a leader?" The way people answer that question can reveal a lot about them and about whether they'll really respond to your leadership style. I like to hear candidates say they expect me to provide the guidelines necessary to do their job, offer sufficient support for them to function capably, and give them the tools and the resources they'll need to be effective. I also evaluate the sincerity and the determination with which candidates answer the question. Obviously, I prefer confident responses to those that look for my approval. A candidate's response can give you great insight into what you can expect from the individual and what his or her leadership style might be.

Another key indicator is a candidate's use of key terms and phrases that provide a tip-off to a leadership style. For example, when someone uses the term "I" much more frequently that "we," I become concerned. I'd rather hear about the accomplishments of a team than those of an individual. I also like to hear about the value a candidate has created for an organization. The manner in which people respond also provides a key to their principles and their managerial approaches. I always say that "we hire brains, not buttons." If I was looking for someone to take orders, I would just need a button to push. When you choose people for key staff positions, you're choosing them because of their intelligence, experience, and their ability to apply these attributes to new challenges. When you gain a leadership role on the staff, you're expected to be an innovator and collaborator, not a follower of directions.

> Trust is not easily earned. It is developed over time through sharing experiences and by working together on a day-to-day basis.

Building an effective team means building trust at all levels. Trust is not easily earned. It is developed over time through sharing experiences and by working together on a day-to-day basis. To build your trust in the people in your organization, you must first help them build trust in you. You need to be open and honest in everything you do. You need to be consistent in your behavior. Your people need to know that you'll be there to back them up should the need arise. Look for ways to display these qualities to your staff as often as you can. In time, you will build a bridge of trust to them.

One of the ways I've earned the trust of my staff is by sharing any and all successes. I very rarely take personal credit for the achievements of my organization, but I always make sure my team receives recognition. Once I had a key staff leader who managed a large part of my organization. We were engaged in an issue that was quite visible to the general public, and leading news services frequently wanted to interview us as "industry experts." This individual insisted on taking all of the interviews herself. I questioned her as to why she did not want any of her staff to take some of "the abuse." She adopted the very self-centered position that, as the leader of the group, she should become its public "face." That single response provided me with insights about the trustworthiness of that individual. As I began to look deeper into her operation and personnel, a profound lack of leadership became apparent. The people in the trenches were not given any latitude to think for themselves or to make decisions; rather, they were dictated to. This was not a healthy recipe for success. I subsequently replaced that individual with a new candidate who was much more in tune with our organizational goals and objectives. That personnel move not only improved my credibility and trust with her group, but with the rest of my organization as well.

In most organizations, people know who is trustworthy and who is not. They expect a leader to know as well, and to take action when necessary. Leaders must become intimately involved in the organization and must always look out for the best interests of the team, even at the expense of an individual. Everyone needs to be trustworthy. Everyone needs to accept responsibilities. Everyone needs to be supportive of the team. If you do not act quickly and decisively with people who fail to adhere to those principles, you will lose the respect and trust of your organization and suffer the consequence of less-than-optimal performance.

It Is Okay to Be Passionate

A large part of leadership involves motivation. In addition to being lighthearted and trustworthy, having a certain amount of passion creates a level of enthusiasm in the organization that is necessary for success. Passion is a contagious emotion; people seem to thrive on passion and excitement. Day-to-day business can become very mundane and routine. To keep people excited, show some passion in everything you do. I don't mean running up and down the halls leading cheers for the team. I mean sincerely demonstrating your commitment to the job you are performing. Strong leadership requires that you believe in what you're doing and believe that it will produce a positive outcome.

When you exhibit a certain amount of passion, people feel much more comfortable about following you and working with you. Life is very uncertain, as we all know, and in the business world many decisions involve risk. I used to call them "mortgage decisions." If I made the right decision, I could pay my mortgage; if I didn't, I'd be in trouble. Passion is part and parcel of such decisions. If people feel that you truly believe in your undertaking, they will go above and beyond the call of duty to support you. Sometimes success requires just that little extra effort, either from you, your subordinates, or your peers. Passion is the engine to generate that effort.

> Having something in our lives that we're passionate about—in addition to our job and family—makes us more successful.

I hope you feel passionately about something outside the workplace. Having something in our lives that we're passionate about—in addition to our job and family—makes us more successful. Our lives require a delicate balance between family, job, and self. Passion plays a big role in helping us maintain that equilibrium. You need to invest a sufficient amount of passion and commitment into each of these areas in order to be successful. Exert too much effort in any one area, and the other two will suffer. The underlying passion you develop in all three areas is a surefire way to create that balance. In the opening of this chapter, I talked about the need to be one person and not a split personality. This holds true here as well. It is hard to be passionate if you are not singularly focused.

Outside work, I've been lucky enough to develop a passion for automobile racing. I think it has made me far more productive as a leader in the corporate world. (It has certainly helped develop my team-building skills.) Racing offers me a release from day-to-day pressures that we all need. On the track I'm totally focused and free from all of the issues at work. This cleansing is quite beneficial. Focusing on a recreational activity for which you have a passion clears the mind and makes your thought processes sharper. My son has shared my passion for racing, and we have been able to race together now for 15 years. To me, that is the best of both worlds—sharing my passion for an outside activity with my son. Life is such a short journey, and we need to make the most of it. Take the time to pursue an activity or a hobby beyond the workplace that excites you, and develop a passion for it. It is an extremely enjoyable way to become a much more effective leader. Passion breeds passion. As a leader it is important to be a motivator as well. If people sense passion in your voice and your actions it will spread to the rest of your organization. Try to come to work each day with the same demeanor, the same level of energy, and the same passion you bring to your activities outside work. I know this is not easy, but building a trusting relationship with your team and with your peers is easier when you bring a high level of passion and excitement to your work. People like to be around people who have passion and a positive attitude.

> Passion breeds passion. As a leader it is important to be a motivator as well. If people sense passion in your voice and your actions it will spread to the rest of your organization.

CHAPTER 5

Soft Stuff Is What Really Matters

The advent of the Internet and the steady change in technology and human behaviors because of it have profoundly affected the way we live our lives, the way we interact with others, and the way we conduct ourselves in the workplace. The ideas of personalization and instant gratification, too, have migrated to the workforce. Together, these changes have profoundly affected how we lead people in our organizations. The management practices of the past no longer apply to today's world. Society has changed and people today expect a more personal touch and a collaborative approach to leadership. There is a soft side to being a leader in today's environment. Just as electronics, medicine, and many other fields have changed profoundly in the last decade, technological advances have introduced profound changes to the meaning of leadership. The differences in the values of different generations of employees are more exaggerated today than at any time I can remember. My generation comes from a more structured and hierarchical world. Organizational structures were like pyramids. Today's organizations are much flatter with larger spans of control and more individual autonomy. What works for the older generation will no longer work for the younger. They expect to be treated as individuals and to have the opportunity to work in a less structured environment. It is important to recognize and embrace these different expectations to be an effective leader in today's workplace.

> What works for the older generation will no longer work for the younger. They expect to be treated as individuals and to have the opportunity to work in a less structured environment.

Many companies are adopting a new approach to the hiring process that emphasizes understanding you as a whole person rather than focusing narrowly on your resume and specific successes from your past. Companies want this holistic view of you before considering you for employment. What they are looking for is key motivating factors; the things about you that made you successful and that align you with the goals and objectives of their company. For example, in the technology field, employers look at how early in your life you actually became involved in technology. According to the people with whom I've spoken, the earlier you become involved, the more favorable people believe your prospects for future success are. It is almost a return to the behavioral testing that was fashionable earlier in my career, except they have changed the emphasis of the test to examine a total behavior model rather than focusing narrowly on identifying a fit for the company's unique culture. Companies today take a much deeper look at you as an individual. In some ways this is a good idea. It is about time that corporations start to think more of us as individuals rather than just boxes on an org chart. Over the years, we became very insensitive to individual needs as management adopted a narrow focus on achieving corporate goals. This approach has also played out in our interactions with each other. We became programmed by a corporate culture that said "It's all about the job; you need to focus on it and it only and worry about your personal relationships and well-being outside of the workplace." The younger generation coming into the workplace today has changed all of that. They will no longer tolerate a static sterile corporate environment. They look at the workday as part of the total life experience and want to have the same types of experiences there that they do outside of the workplace.

The Generation Gap

Many of us have looked at the younger generation with a critical eye, but I firmly believe they have the right idea about the need to integrate their personal and professional lives. They understand that the job is a part of your life, not all of your life, and they choose not to compromise themselves or their lives for the job. I grew up in an environment where my father had a single job for over 30 years. He worked in the same railroad his entire career. My father-in-law delivered bread to grocery stores and worked for the same company for his entire career. Every time I have changed jobs, both of them have looked at me and said, "What are you crazy? You have great benefits where you are; why would you ever want to leave?" Our feelings toward the company and the job changed between my generation and my father's generation. When I first started out in corporate life working for IBM, I expected to have a job for life. In most government jobs you were guaranteed tenure for your entire career. All of a sudden the economic climate changed and IBM, governments, and many other employers started laying people off. This profoundly affected the younger generation. They saw the stress put on their parents and the influence it had on their day-to-day lives. This led them to develop a more cynical view of corporations than that of their parents.

I can remember for many years having staff in Europe and visiting the continent are seeing how different their approach to work was. There are several problems as I write this with countries in Europe regarding the role of governments in the finances of those countries, but I really believe they found the essence of life a lot sooner than we did. It took our younger generation to begin to educate us. People today work to live rather than living to work, and this shift explains the changes we are seeing in our marketplace and our workplace today. For years, the Europeans had a totally different approach to work than we did with longer vacations, more time off, more support from the government for employee benefits, and a work ethic that resulted in fewer hours worked than in the United States. Their approach may be more extreme than the balanced approach we are seeking today, but they had the right idea before we did. In the United States we have finally reached more of a balance between the workplace and our personal lives. The younger generation of workers has a better understanding of where their careers begin and end. They see their careers as only a small part of their lives and are not willing to make the time commitments older workers did throughout their careers. They have a more holistic view of life than their older peers. When you look back over recent history it is always the younger generation that drives change in our society.

I served in the military during the Vietnam conflict and experienced the antiwar sentiment of the younger generation and the demonstrations on college campuses. At the time I was bitter. Having a chance to look back over many years, I think historians will write, "They understood the situation for what it was, and they had a different perspective than we did." I was drafted into the military and had to have a positive outlook about why I was serving my country. To this day I'm still extremely proud to have been in the service of our country; however, I do feel that our government and our politicians have engaged us in conflicts where we should not have had any involvement. The younger generation has been recognizing this for decades now and usually it is their grassroots efforts that drive social change. I think a lot of it is because they haven't been tainted by the politics of corporations and the politics of day-to-day life. They have a fresh and unbiased perspective on the world that allows them to see things a little more clearly than we do. I'm not saying they are right in every case, but a lot of the positive social change that has come about in the United States and other countries has been created by the young. We all tend to forget that we were young once ourselves.

Combining Cultures

The social changes going on inside of our corporations today are a result of this useful movement toward a better balance of the professional and the personal. We need to adapt to the expectations of the younger generation in order to be successful both as companies and as leaders. We need to understand their expectations and balance them with the goals of the corporation. We also need to do this in a way that does not alienate employees from earlier generations. Finding that balance is the type of soft skills successful leaders demonstrate. The best leaders are the ones who recognize these intricacies and have been able to create an environment of balance between multiple generations working together.

> We need to adapt to the expectations of the younger generation in order to be successful both as companies and as leaders.

I try to address this issue in multiple ways. One way is to create mixed generational teams whenever possible. The agile methodology for project management allows managers to create this type of environment. It fosters intrateam discussion and encourages people to speak their minds and contribute ideas. This structure allows me to build cohesive teams incorporating members from multiple generations. This environment also allows these teams to learn from each other and create a combined culture. It is this combined culture that allows us to succeed as an organization.

Another lesson that I learned trying to work with multiple generations is to never forget where I came from as an individual. I will sit in the cubicles of people in my organization and ask them how many ceiling tiles they have above their cubicle. They look at me for a while and all of a sudden smile. I tell them I remember when I was sitting in the same place, when we used to count the ceiling tiles above our cubicles and see who had the most tiles. These little games helped us build a culture back then. The same things hold true today. Although we have different generations and different perspectives, we are motivated by a lot of the same things. We want to know that we are treated fairly, that we have an equal opportunity to succeed, and that the corporation will recognize our efforts. An important way for a leader today to achieve these goals is to remember earlier personal experiences and how they helped you grow as an individual. When thinking about these experiences, remember what makes them important and how they helped you mold yourself to the cultures and the teams with which you have worked. Most importantly is to also remember how you thought, what was important to you, what motivated you, and what you expected of the corporation. These are all critical factors in creating your foundation as a leader to better understand the motivations of your team and to bring them together. Many doors will open to you when the people in your organization understand that you are human, that you have had the same experiences they have, that you have sat in their chair and appreciate what they are going through, and that you are willing to bring yourself to their level and work with them as a team to help you all gain success. This unselfish effort on your part creates respect and admiration for your leadership among your team members. Never forget the soft stuff.

Match Your Style to the Market

In order to be an effective leader, you need to ensure that your style is comparable to the expectations of the marketplace. The best leaders I've known have been able to modify their style such that they can effectively take advantage of changes in market conditions. The ones I've known who have not been successful have not. There is an old saying that goes "You can't be a stiff tree in a strong breeze" and that holds true in this environment as well. Holding on to the old ways will not allow you to be successful in today's world. You need to be able to bend and be flexible to modify your behavior, skills, and approach to business in a way that better aligns you with the world today. This is a phenomenon that is not going to change. If anything, it will increase its velocity over time. As we have discussed many times, the pace of change is continuing to increase every year. That change affects the way we lead. We can see this from generation to generation. The expectations of today's young people entering the marketplace are totally different from those of their predecessors. Because of these changes, the ways we motivate and lead younger employees are totally different from the ways we used to motivate our employees in the past. People today are driven more by individual satisfaction than by a desire to achieve corporate goals. They view the world in a totally different way than we did as we started our careers. The turmoil that has undertaken corporations over the years with multiple layoffs, organizational changes, upsizing, and downsizing has created a whole new culture among employees. Corporate loyalty seems to be a thing of the past and is being replaced with a more personalized approach to people's careers. Most people today look at their jobs as a business relationship with their employer, and they see this relationship as a two-way street. The foundation of this relationship between employee and company is the match between the needs of each. As long as these needs remain in balance an employee is happy and the company is happy. When things get out of balance, an adjustment needs to be made. Employees view it as a black-and-white relationship: as long as they are happy with the opportunity the company is providing them, they will stay. Companies believe that as long as the company is getting the services from the employee that it expects it will retain them. The company–employee relationship seems to be more in the moment than in the longer term vision as it was years ago. Understanding this and understanding how it affects leadership is extremely important as you develop your leadership style with this new generation.

> Holding on to the old ways will not allow you to be successful in today's world. You need to be able to bend and be flexible to modify your behavior, skills, and approach to business in a way that better aligns you with the world today.

As leaders, we are often caught up in day-to-day activities and never really take time to reflect on these types of issues. These soft issues, rather than the hard ones, will gain you more success as a leader. Soft stuff will get you promoted faster than hard stuff. We need to realign our priorities as leaders to focus more of our attention on these types of issues. The expectations of today's workforce and the teamwork that is so important in today's corporations require us to pay more attention to these soft skills. People are more motivated by emotion today than they have ever been before.

Today's leaders need to get out of their offices more. They need to manage by wandering. The perception of success as a leader today may be more about the personal touch and its effects on your organization than on having processes and procedures in place that will directly affect the success of your organization. I have a style of managing by wandering. I allocate a certain portion of every day to walking around and talking to my people and to anyone else I happen to pass in the hallway. This is an important strategy to build those soft relationships within my organization and within the company at large.

> I allocate a certain portion of every day to walking around and talking to my people and to anyone else I happen to pass in the hallway. This is an important strategy to build those soft relationships within my organization and within the company at large.

Today's trends toward personalization have also had a significant impact on the expectations of leaders. When I was in the Army everything was structured. Everything we did was pre-planned even down to the uniform of the day. We were told when to eat, when to sleep, what to wear, and how to behave: as GIs and not as individuals. The approach was "if one fails, we all fail"; that we were all integral to the team and we all had to make equal contributions. If someone was unable to make contributions, it was our responsibility to fill in and make up for that. This type of approach worked well then based on the cultural values we shared as a society. We were coming from a heavy industrial age where everyone followed process standards and rules. We were just beginning the migration from a workplace built around industrialized processes to a workplace built around intellectual labor. If you take a look at soldiers in today's Army, the way they are governed is totally different than when I was in the military. Soldiers are expected today to think and act as individuals and sometimes even to question authority. This was totally unheard of during my tenure in the military. This is a glaring example of the change in societal behavior that has been undertaken in the last few decades. This type of change has been even more profound in the corporate world.

I have talked to many leaders over the years who claim never to have time to get out of their offices to visit with peers, network, or join professional organizations. They always say they are too busy and just can't get away from their day-to-day work activities. In many cases, the next call I get from them is to tell me they have lost their job. They never saw it coming, never thought it would happen to them, but it did. For these types of leaders, the job to them meant what I would call the hard stuff: the execution of their responsibilities, the completion of projects at hand, managing to their budgets, and running the day-to-day operation. Of course, the hard aspects of your job are very important. You need to execute on a daily basis, to bring things in on time and on budget, but it is not the only aspect of your job. Too many leaders are focused exclusively on the hard parts and ignore the rest.

> A leader totally focused on deadlines and delivery schedules cannot provide the leadership workers from this new generation are seeking.

Today's world is a different environment that it was 10 or 15 years ago. In today's world it is more about the people and relationships, collaboration, and teamwork. This is a profound change in corporate culture and in social culture. The new generations entering our workforce have a far different perspective about work than those that preceded them. They are motivated by self-fulfillment more than by delivering on the expectations of the corporation. Their emphasis is on their individual careers rather than the organizations for which they work. A leader totally focused on deadlines and delivery schedules cannot provide the leadership workers from this new generation are seeking.

Ego Gets You Fired

Through my years of racing I spent a lot of time observing the behaviors of my fellow competitors. You would think the most successful racecar drivers are the ones who are the most intense and overly competitive. I found just the opposite. The most successful drivers I have seen in years of competition have been the ones who are laid back, calculating, and decisive in their actions. Rather than reacting, they analyze the situation, size up the variables, and make a decision. I know this sounds rather funny when you are going 170 miles an hour, but it is true. They also have a generally laid-back attitude. I definitely never sense a lot of ego in them; however, I did in some of the more unsuccessful drivers. What the successful drivers display is a calculated propensity to be the best at what they do, to compete fairly, and to let the outcome speak for them. The ones with the egos tend to be the ones who spin out on the first lap and always have excuses for their lack of performance. They blame the equipment; they blame the other drivers; they blame the track conditions; they blame the weather. There is always an excuse for their inability to perform, but the root the problem is that their ego won't allow them to win.

Ego is a funny thing. In a racecar, if you know you are racing drivers with large egos they are very easy to beat. All you need to do is psych them out. Get in their mirrors and show them you are there, and swing from side to side, and get right on the rear bumper, and draft them, and even bump draft them: anything to make them uncomfortable. The drivers with large egos don't know how to deal with this. Successful drivers ignore this type of harassment and instead stick to the game plan, find their lines, and know their breaking points. Their attitude is "I'll be fine, and if I'm not he'll pass me, I'll find out why he's faster than me, and I'll pass him back."

I can remember another occasion when I was first getting into racing when one of the other drivers would walk to the false grid with his umbrella in tow to shade him from the hot sun while his crew pushed the car over where he would immediately get in his car, get strapped in, and put on his helmet. The green flag would drop and that is when his courage would end. It was all about the bravado, the show before the race, the attention. The best drivers I know arrive unceremoniously, help push their car, and then walk around and chat with the other drivers. They enjoy the experience before strapping themselves into the cars to start racing. They are the ones who are there for the checkered flag at the end of the race.

This same phenomenon is also true in corporate life. I've seen many bloated egos in my career. I can remember one instance where I was working for a multibillion-dollar corporation and I was charged with the merger of a $2 billion acquisition. This was an interesting experience. We had two companies with differing cultures, differing technologies, and differing styles of management. I remember one executive in the company we had acquired would never attend my meetings. It seemed he had determined that I was a level below him and he would not attend my meetings unless someone else in the room was at his level. This was ego to the nth degree. I confronted him. He said he felt it was important that he had people of equal stature in the room because he had spent his career achieving his current status. He wanted to make sure he was dealing with people at a similar level. Well, the rest of the story is that within six months of the merger he was gone and I was still there. His ego got him fired. He never took the time to understand the new culture we were trying to create, to understand the interactions of our management team, or to adjust himself to the new situation. I can't stress enough that it is important for all of us not to get caught up in our personal egos but rather to assess the situation we are in and understand the feelings of those around us.

There was one point in my career when I was a CIO of a high-growth high-tech company. I was recruited from a position in Florida to move back up to New Jersey and assume the role. I remember it was an exhaustive process with all of the personality tests corporations used to perform. One funny note was that while I was taking my personality testing in Florida the power went out and I was sitting there with the psychologist who was testing me and the room kept getting warmer and warmer. I was in a full suit with a tie and I tend to sweat quite a bit; needless to say, that day I was sweating profusely. I remember the psychologist telling me we were behind closed doors, so I could make myself more comfortable without worrying it would affect the results of the test. Needless to say, I did not shed a stitch, and I felt that was part of the test as well. I think I lost three pounds of fluids from sweating, but I made my point. It is interesting how you react when you are in different situations; you tend to gravitate toward caution more than the situation requires.

We had built a whole new executive team at this corporation. One of the perks we had was access to a company driver whenever we were going back and forth to the airport or into New York City. We had two cars, a Cadillac limousine and a Mercedes limousine. I really didn't care which vehicle I used and I was only happy I had a perk that provided a driver to take me where I needed to go. This was an experience I had never had in my life before. Honestly, I was somewhat in awe of it, and I never stopped appreciating it. I remember a vice president of sales, he was from Canada, who had a bit of an ego, and was developing a reputation of being somewhat distant. One day when we were sitting in an operating committee meeting discussing plans for the future he was talking about an upcoming road trip when he would be on the road making several appearances around the country to try to boost sales. After the meeting he called the driver to go to the airport, and the driver showed up with the Cadillac limousine. He was incensed the driver had chosen the Cadillac limousine over the Mercedes to take him to the airport. He made it quite clear to the driver that he would only ride in the Mercedes limousine and not the Cadillac and that this should never happen again. I was watching the face of our driver, whose name was Bob, and I could see by the expression on his face he was thinking "What is wrong with you? What does it matter what vehicle I drive when I'm here to drive you to the airport?" Being new to the executive team and not having experienced this type of behavior before, I couldn't help wondering to myself what was motivating this kind of behavior. To this day, I'm just grateful that I had a driver to take me wherever I wanted to go; it didn't matter to me what I was riding in. This was the first time in my corporate career I ever experienced that level of egotistical behavior driving someone's decisions. As in the previous example, it wasn't long before he lost his job as well.

When you move up the corporate ladder you gain more and more perks. Don't think it is all about you. Always remember the perks go with the position rather than the person. Once you vacate a position and leave the corporation the position transfers to someone else. So many times I've witnessed my peers' egos grow with the number of perks associated with a position. It is hard not to have a large ego when you are treated the way you are at the top of corporate America today, but you always need to remember: It is not about you; it is about the position. Don't get caught in that same trap. Appreciate all the perks you have when you have them. Enjoy them and use them as much as you possibly can. But don't let it go to your head. There is enough jealousy in the corporation from the people beneath you who don't have all of the perks you may have, so don't add further fuel to that fire by being egotistical about it.

The biggest lesson I learned from these experiences is that ego is not a positive emotion. Through my entire corporate career I have never seen anyone succeed through ego. Ego only alienates you from others. Your will to succeed gets you ahead. There is a profound difference between ego and will to succeed. Will to succeed means that you are a driven person, you have higher expectations for yourself and those with whom you work, and you are willing to make sacrifices to gain success. The key delineator between ego and will to succeed is that someone with a will to succeed is always reaching out to others to help them in their journey. A person with ego goes it alone. Having a will to succeed is a positive emotion. It shows that you have passion for what you do, and are driven to continually improve yourself and those around you. It is okay to be impatient with others, but at the end of the day success is gained through teamwork rather than through individual effort.

> The key delineator between ego and will to succeed is that someone with a will to succeed is always reaching out to others to help them in their journey. A person with ego goes it alone.

Be a Good Communicator

Effective communication is probably one the most important aspects of racing. Whether we are in a test session qualifying or during the race, I am in constant communication with my crew. When you are driving a racecar and dealing with all of the other outside stimuli you need that backup team behind you to help you gain an objective understanding about what is going on. I am constantly giving the crew feedback on the car and its performance. Whether it is a high-speed entry push or exit over-steer or a car that is just too tight, my crew and I are constantly chattering back and forth to gain an understanding of how we can improve the vehicle and change the outcome of the race. We speak an abbreviated language during the race because we have little time to communicate with each other as the action is fast and furious. This is something we also need to do in the workplace. We need to develop our own language and our own style as communicators so we can effectively communicate with our team.

I race as part of a three-car team, and each one of us requires a different setup from a car because each one of us has his own preferences. Despite these differences, we all communicate with our crew and team using the same language. We all use the same terminology so we are as well understood as possible. When you are in a racecar going at an extremely high rate of speed you are excited and you need to remind yourself that you need to slow down and communicate clearly; otherwise, the team may misunderstand what you are saying. This holds true in corporate life as well. We need to make sure that the manner in which we communicate ensures people will easily understand the message we are trying to convey. Racing has taught me the art of clear, concise, and honest communication, and I've applied this lesson throughout my corporate career.

We all spend our careers honing our skills. We are constantly reading to keep up to date and finding other ways to improve ourselves. Surely these are the things you need to do to become successful in a chosen career; however, they don't really address the softer issues discussed in this chapter. It is always good to know that you are proficient in the skills of your profession, but we tend to overlook good communication as one of those skills. Many of the executives I have worked with and observed through the years have been terrible communicators. It doesn't do much good for you to hone your skills and hone your capabilities if you are unable to communicate effectively with those around you. A common trait in a lot of leaders is that they are introverts, even though they are in the public eye and give presentations on a regular basis. This is something we all deal with from time to time, but in a leadership career it is important to realize there is a time to be left alone but there is also a time when you need to be out in front of your team and communicating with them on a regular basis. We tend to assume that our communication with others is sufficient. In most cases it is not. There are very few cases in which you can over-communicate in corporate America today. People tend to develop insecurities and misperceptions based on lack of communication from their leaders.

As I have developed my leadership skills through my career, I have come to understand that communication is one of the most important requirements to becoming an effective leader. People always want to know where you stand and they want to know what you think of them and their performance. The worst leaders are those who perform annual reviews and highlight their concerns with an employee's behavior over the past year. They might talk about something that happened three, four, or five months ago in an annual review. I find this to be poor leadership. As I've said elsewhere, being a leader is like raising children. A good leader highlights good or bad behavior when it happens. It doesn't do you much good to tell your children about something they did wrong last week. You need to react to it at the time it happens rather than wait. This is the only way you can positively influence their behavior. The same holds true in corporate life. If you find something either good or bad in an employee's behavior it is imperative that you address it at that time rather than waiting for some later date. I think a lot of us do this because we are uncomfortable in situations that require us to provide feedback. In order to be a successful leader you need to move beyond that discomfort and be able to have honest and timely communications with your staff. You'll find over time that you gain more support from your team than you ever could have imagined by just communicating in a timely and honest manner.

It is imperative that you communicate regularly with your peers as well. The best communicators are the ones who take the initiative to reach out to others rather than sitting back and waiting to be approached. Just like friendship, you need to be the one willing to take the initiative in order to become a good peer to your colleagues. The more you learn to communicate with your peers the more information you are going to gather from them. You'd be surprised how much you can learn over lunch with one of your peers. Always try to put them at ease when you are communicating with them as they will be much more receptive to what you are trying to say when they are relaxed.

> You'll find over time that you gain more support from your team than you ever could have imagined by just communicating in a timely and honest manner.

In general, corporations today are terrible communicators. It is imperative on us as leaders to foster an environment that generates more effective communication. This is something that we all talk about but do very little. If you look at the most successful corporations today they have a culture of openness, honesty, and free communication. This is the type of environment younger people coming into corporate America are looking for. In the old world everyone was afraid to say something for fear of getting into trouble. We need to break down those barriers and move toward a more collegial environment where people are free to say and do what they feel is right for both themselves and the corporation without fear of being persecuted for it. This starts with a company's leaders. We need to overcome that fear ourselves and be able to communicate openly with others without worrying about fear of retribution. I'm not saying that we should communicate everything and anything; some things may be detrimental to ourselves, to the corporation, or to others. What I am saying, though, is that the more we set an example of open communication, the more we create that communicative culture within our organization.

The best foundation for becoming a good communicator is honesty. Always tell the truth, and if you are not sure don't say it. The same holds true for corporations. They need to be open and honest as they communicate with others. People are not easily fooled. They understand when leaders are holding back or corporations are reluctant to give relevant information. We need to break down these barriers to be as open and honest as we possibly can. As I said before, there are certain things we cannot say; however, let's make sure we don't constantly try to hide behind an unnecessary desire for secrecy that prevents us from communicating clearly and openly.

> The best foundation for becoming a good communicator is honesty. Always tell the truth, and if you are not sure don't say it.

These are the soft skills we need to constantly practice at home and work if we wish to be effective leaders. People respond to people they like to be around, people they trust, and people they feel comfortable around. It is not just about mandating anymore in corporate America, it is about being able to influence behavior and actions in a positive way. This can only be accomplished by leaders who understand this and take the time to develop the soft skills necessary for success.

CHAPTER 6

How Do You Compete?

After several days of preparation and tweaking, turning several laps, reading all the computer telemetry, and timing sessions, it is now time for the race. This is the time your adrenaline starts running, your heart starts pumping, your blood pressure goes up a little bit, and you start going over the track in your mind. Now it is time to get in the car, get strapped down, put on your Hans device, get connected to your radio, and put on your gloves and your game face. You are now ready for the parade lap and one rotation around the track scrubbing your tires in, checking your radio, tracking everything, checking your belts, making sure things are working properly, and getting ready for the start of the race. The drivers cross over and double up as we approach the turn. It is now time for us to line up and make a right-hand turn onto the straight. Your heart is pounding so hard you can feel it in your neck, and you can feel the adrenaline rushing through your body. It is time to plan where you want to go when the green flag drops. The team leader is watching the starter for the flag to drop. He has the transmission button pushed with an open microphone so he can give the command—GREEN! GREEN! GREEN!

When the flag drops, it is total chaos for a couple seconds as everyone tries to see what you are doing, to find that little hole to gain a position on everyone else. Everyone seems to head for the inside of turn one, which creates a huge traffic jam, but my teammates and I always like to go around the outside. Not only does this usually allow us to pick up four or five positions, we also avoid the chaos on the inside. It never ceases to amaze me how many major wrecks happen on the first turn of every race. I guess it is because all racers are so competitive that they just can't wait for the next corner. They want to win on the first.

Competing on the Job Is Not Enough

When I was learning to drive, I went to a school. The instructor pulled a short length of rope from his sleeve. He said, "This is the first turn." He then pulled the rest of the rope out and said, "This is the rest of the race. If you wreck on the first turn, you never get to finish the rest of the race." Having said that, the first turn is the best opportunity to gain multiple positions. You just have to be aggressive but constantly aware of what is unfolding around you. Successfully negotiating the first turn requires the same ability to balance short-term gains and long-term strategy necessary to successfully compete in business.

After clearing the first turn, you settle down, get into a rhythm, and focus on the person in front of you. It is now time to set them up for the pass. The most fun of racing is discovering where another driver is faster than you, finding where you are faster than him or her, and then planning a strategy to pass. One of the things I always try to do is get on the gas just before the person in front of me as we leave a corner. You can actually hear another driver get on the throttle. If I can get to the gas a second faster than the person in front of me, I can be much faster coming out of the corner, giving me the momentum and opportunity to pass. Racing, just like corporate life, is a strategy game, and the goal is to both outthink and outperform your competition. I guess that is why I enjoy it so much.

It is all about you, the machine, the people around you, and many other variables in your mind. I know it sounds like just an extension of the workday, but it really isn't. For me, it's a chance to release all the pent-up pressure that built during the work week. That release is all we need now and then to survive in the corporate world.

Racing, for me, is a good way to hone my competitive skills and my mental and physical agility. They say that driving a racecar you burn more calories than any other form of exercise. Racing is not only physically demanding, it is also mentally challenging. You can't afford to have your attention lapse for even a second. You need to be aware of everything that is going on around you all the time. The interesting thing about the mental challenge of racing is that while you are driving your mind is often telling you one thing and the racecar is telling you another. My mind is often telling me I'm going too fast for this corner and I am not going to make it while the racecar is telling me I can make it through without a problem. You go through a constant mental battle with yourself during the entire competition. Couple that with the fact that you are trying to look for your break points, your turning points, and your entry speeds or exit speeds, as well as planning how to pass the driver in front of you while preventing the drivers behind you from passing. All of these things together create an environment that requires an extreme mental workout. The reason I mention this is because a lot of people say the mind is a lot like a muscle: If you don't exercise it, if you don't challenge it, it deteriorates. Competition is one way of keeping your mind sharp. I specifically like my professional racing career because it has provided perspective on my life in business and given me the ability to make decisions with more clarity.

For several years, I raced in the same paddock with Paul Newman. I watched him over the years and his mind always stayed sharp. I believe he was 83 years old when he had his final race. I have to tell you that he probably was just as fast at 83 as he was at 63. Watching him continue to compete and excel at the sport over the years was an eye-opening experience for me. It was his desire to compete and his ability to rise to the mental challenge that allowed him to be successful both on and off the track. I found him a personal inspiration and used to enjoy discussions with him. It was obvious to me watching him through the years that it is all about the regularity of competition, and that the desire to compete helps you build a strong mental foundation for your life.

Racing is a fairly intense form of competition, but there are many other ways each of us can find outlets to hone our competitive skills and build that mental foundation. It can be as easy as putting together a puzzle on the table. Challenge yourself to see how fast you can complete the puzzle. Build your way up from easier puzzles to more difficult puzzles and then to the highly complex puzzles. That is just one example of how you can compete with yourself and with others. The funny thing about it is while we are doing it we don't really realize that we are being competitive because it is something we enjoy doing. It feels good to us, and we can even feel relaxed while we are working on a challenge. You need to include competitive outlets in your day to become the successful person you want to be.

One of the best ways I know to hone your competitive skills is through interactions with your family. When I was raising my children, I never missed an opportunity to play football with my son in the backyard, to work on a craft project with my daughter, or to take walks in the woods with my entire family. The subtle things help you build that competitive foundation you need, and they help you build a bond with your family. I can't think of a better way to improve your personal competitiveness than to participate in family functions as much as you possibly can. These are the types of foundational experiences you can take with you throughout your entire life. Being a parent is a competition. You compete with the outside influences of the world, you compete with your own experiences, and you compete with the differing personalities of your children. Sounds a lot like work, doesn't it? I've always pushed the people who work for me to be engaged as much as they possibly can in the community and with their families because these are the types of experiences that help them gain a better perspective on the world and a better competitive foundation.

It Isn't Just about Winning

Competition doesn't mean you have to win every time. Some of the most useful lessons we learn in life come from those competitions we fail to win. As a businessman and entrepreneur, I've been driven to learn more from the opportunities I have lost than from the opportunities I have won. It is easy to look at the wins and analyze them; it is much more difficult to look at the losses and be open-minded and understand from a competitive perspective what I did well, where the competition excelled, and what I need to change to improve. I spend a good deal of time analyzing those lost cases, but this time is well spent if it prepares me for future challenges. The basic questions I try to answer when I analyze a failure include:

- Why was the competition better in this case?
- What were the gaps I need to fill in the future?
- Was I really prepared for the opportunity or challenge at hand?

- Was I open-minded enough to really understand the realities of my offering?

> Competition doesn't mean you have to win every time. Some of the most useful lessons we learn in life come from those competitions we fail to win.

Being competitive means being open-minded and honest with your team. It is always easy to make excuses when things don't work out the way we expect them to. It takes a strong leader to remain open-minded and honest when evaluating why things didn't work out as planned. I have always found it easy to bring in an uninterested third-party and ask him or her to look at the situation and help me understand what I or my team could have done better or what we were missing in our model. I am constantly challenging my partner to point out when we convinced ourselves we were better than the competition without really taking the time to analyze our offerings in an open-minded comparison to theirs. Too often we get too close to situations and they become so personal that our internal biases cloud our judgment and interfere with our ability to compete successfully.

Being competitive means being honest with yourself. Daily life in a corporation is like being in a racecar where your mind and the car are sending different messages that you need to decipher and integrate in order to succeed. I have found through the years that the most competitive leaders and teams at the most competitive companies are the ones who perform the most research about their competition. They have a thorough understanding of the difference between the value they provide and that provided by their competition. The best sales representatives in the world are the ones who can't wait for you to ask questions because they have already researched answers and have them ready for you. It is this preparation, this understanding of the competition's offering and of your offering, this understanding of your value proposition versus the rest of the field that gives winning companies the edge over others.

Instill Competition in Your Organization

Competition is not a spectator sport; it is a part of our daily lives. This is the type of winning attitude that needs to be instilled in your organization. The reason that we exist as companies, departments, and teams is to beat the competition. If we can't create products and services and infrastructure technologies that provide value when compared to those created by our competitors, we can't survive. That fact is why it is important for leaders to understand the culture at our company, the culture at competing companies, and how to mold and shape our teams, products, and services in a way that gives us a competitive advantage. There are very few applications technology packages in the marketplace today, so most companies are using similar technologies to produce, distribute, and sell their products. The companies that succeed are the ones that can find unique ways to integrate and implement these technologies to produce a superior product. I tell my teams we are "just another white car going down the road." What we need to do is make ourselves better so that we are the white car customers pick out of that line. That is a very unique challenge in today's world. Differentiation between products and services is becoming increasingly blurred as shared technologies appear across supply chains and client bases. That is why competition becomes increasingly important as we consider the internal infrastructures and models we build for our company. We need to find the unique characteristic that differentiates us and makes us better than our competitors or more desirable to our customers.

> We need to find the unique characteristic that differentiates us and makes us better than our competitors or more desirable to our customers.

Successful leaders are the ones who recognize these competitive requirements and rise to the occasion to find ways they can improve their organizations. You can't sit back and wait for someone else to do it for you. I've spoken with many leaders over the years and they tell me they don't receive enough respect, they aren't invited to the meetings that are important, and they never seem to be part of the decision-making process. The reason is because they don't want to compete, to take that extra step, to come up with the innovative ideas or collaborative strategies to work with the rest of the management team and create some value. Competition starts with the individual and spreads to the team. If you are not ready to take the initiative, you will never have the respect of your team and the rest of the corporation.

Controlled Aggression

I have raced with the same team for several years now. We have a three-car team of my son, me, and a third teammate. Every year we do a rebuild of our cars, stripping them down, repainting them, and checking every nut and bolt before putting them back together. One of the things we like to do is make them all look as identical as possible. The one differentiator we always use is that each one of our roll bars is a different color. This difference allows the crew to identify which of us is going by when we are passing them. Sometimes they still get us confused. One time I walked into the shop and when I stopped and looked at my son's car, he had added a decal with the words "Controlled Aggression" to the front of his car and a second, smaller version inside his cockpit. At first I didn't think much about it, but as I reflected over the next couple days, I thought it was a brilliant way to think about competition. Competition is all about winning, about being better, faster, and cheaper in a way that can be repeated. Just running wildly around doesn't get you anywhere. Competition needs to be precisely targeted, well thought out, and always within controlled limits, whether those limits are the result of mental limits, physical limits, or documented controls.

Competition needs to have an objective. We don't just create companies and create products with no strategy, purpose, or expectation in mind. It is always about sizing up the competition. You always know the driver who breaks a little earlier than everyone else, who breaks a little later than everyone else, who is faster going into corners, or who is faster coming out of corners. You know the ones who will block you and the ones who will not block you. These are the kinds of nuances you have to understand about your competitors in order to defeat them. It isn't just about going on the track and going as fast as you can while trying to pass everybody, it is about controlling that aggression and understanding the competition and the environment and doing the research needed so that when you have an opportunity you are ready to strike. If you look at successful companies, one trait they share is that they aren't simply aggressive—they are aggressive in controlled way that allow them to focus and excel.

> If you look at successful companies, one trait they share is that they aren't simply aggressive—they are aggressive in controlled way that allows them to focus and excel.

When my son and I first started our professional racing careers, I took second place behind him a lot. Being older and wiser, I recognized that, while he was winning races, his aggression was not controlled and I could exploit that to beat him. As we would compete in different venues during subsequent races, he would go out and attack the racecourse with vim, vigor, and uncontrolled aggression. By the end of the second, third, or fourth lap, I could see that his tires were wearing out faster than mine, and I'd watch that and get faster bit by bit until I was able to pass him on many occasions because I had more control over the car by the time I made my move. Success isn't just about being fast, it is about being faster through planning and using your resources in a controlled way. The bad news is he learned this lesson very fast and I have yet to beat him since, but it was a lesson that was well learned that I was able to exploit.

It is good to be competitive and aggressive in our daily lives, but we need to always take a step back and ask whether our aggression is under control and whether we are controlling the situation. Are you the one setting the standards for the situation, or you wandering aimlessly and succeeding by luck? In today's world decisions are made at an increasingly rapid pace. We find ourselves constantly trying to keep abreast of progress by companies that are our competitors. This is why many of us do not take the time to fully understand the situation in a controlled manner as we build our competitive plans. We all feel that we need to react, to do something, for fear that failure to act means we will lose. Sometimes no action at all is the best course, but in all cases a calculated, controlled, and aggressive reaction will get you much further than a haphazard and unplanned one.

Do not confuse controlled aggression with analysis paralysis. Being controlled and being calculating in a competitive environment requires you to assess the situation, understand the plan, and act on it quickly and effectively at the opportune moment. Many of us take calculation to an extreme and find ourselves studying the situation and never being able to effectively react to it. As I will mention in Chapter 8, I have a friend who uses the expression "striving and never arriving." It is this balance between understanding the needs of the situation, putting together a controlled and aggressive plan to address the situation, and doing it in an effective manner that allows you to come to resolution ahead of the competition. Each one of us has an internal safety switch that makes us feel increasingly comfortable the more we study things because studying things means you don't have to make a decision. Being a controlled aggressor means having the courage to analyze the situation as much as necessary before taking the next important step and making a decision. We've all heard the expression "the worst decision you can make is no decision at all," and this is particularly true in the competitive world of business. You have to maintain a balance between analysis, understanding, and research and the aggressive decision making necessary to beat the competition. That is what I would call "controlled aggression."

> Sometimes no action at all is the best course, but in all cases a calculated, controlled, and aggressive reaction will get you much further than a haphazard and unplanned one.

Politics

Like it or not, politics is a part of our daily lives. Politics isn't just about the political landscape. It is those things that define how we interact with others: differences in our personalities, perceptions, backgrounds, and experiences. Everyone looks at politics as a "necessary evil" when really it is about learning how to adapt your actions to address the actions of those around you. Political interactions don't need to produce a winner or loser as they must in electoral politics. As we see on TV and read in the newspapers describing our current economic situation, a lot of politics is about compromise and personal interaction.

Politics and competition are intertwined. In most cases, we interact with others because we anticipate a particular outcome. That may be swaying them to a decision we prefer, convincing them of the viability of a product or service, or gaining their assistance in achieving our goals. These are all competitive engagements. Our objective in each of these interactions is to achieve the outcome we desire by employing the resources of others. You do not have to be manipulative to be politically astute. You do need to be someone who takes the time to understand the reference points, backgrounds, and positions of those with whom you are interacting and use that understanding to achieve a favorable outcome.

In order to have success in competition, you need to better understand those you are competing against. Those who find politics unsavory, uncomfortable, and personally threatening don't understand that each of us has political motivations and a personal political agenda different from the agenda of anyone else. The successful people in business understand that everyone has an agenda, whether or not they always agree with the point of view or objectives it incorporates. They also understand that gaining an intimate knowledge of what matters to the competition allows them to achieve their goals with the support and understanding of others. This is a critical talent that effective leaders need to develop.

> In order to have success in competition you need to better understand those you are competing against.

We all want to win in every situation. We all believe that our perceptions, views, and concepts are the best, and we

110

sometimes have trouble understanding why others can't comprehend our point of view. So what do most of us do? We sometimes tend to go it alone as we feel that we have a better understanding of the situation than our peers. We tend to circumvent what I would call the political process. I always explain to corporate leaders that when you take yourself out of the political process by not competing you often find yourself at the end of a branch and as you look back everyone else has saws in hand. Going it alone and trying to implement what you believe is the best solution without challenging that belief through exposure to other ideas does not make you a strong competitor. What it does is narrow your thinking and create an environment of animosity with your peers. Trying to force decisions by eliminating competition creates two problems. You will lack the support of your peers in achieving your success criteria in the current project and should things go wrong or not completely according to plan, you will lack support to help you address the problems and turn around a troubled project. In both cases you are left at the end of that branch with no support and no easy means of climbing down. This is a hard lesson for many of us to learn as we tend to become impatient and just want to get the job finished rather than take the time to engage with others. This can hurt you in two ways: You get a reputation of not being a team player and you never learn the art of delegation. The more you force yourself to include others, the more you will find that you end up with the best possible solution to the current problem. You have not only shown your team spirit, but you may also have learned something new from the other members of your team in the process.

This reminds me of a leader I met a couple of years ago. During a discussion, she mentioned to me that the biggest obstacle to a success for her corporation was a lack of an effective portal for the client population. She was determined to construct a new portal that she felt was more like similar service offerings from her competitors. I asked her why she was so passionate about it. She told me it was because it was obvious it was the one critical factor to success of her company that had not been fulfilled. The next question I asked her was who else supported a new portal. Her answer was that most of the leaders of the company just didn't seem to get it. She had been talking to them for a long period of time, and receiving a warm response, but no one seemed particularly interested. I asked her if she had any support at all for this initiative with the company. Her answer was that most of the people in her department and her organization agreed with her. I then asked her to put together a presentation of the value proposition of this new portal and what it would be to the company as well as how it would allow the company to better perform against the competition. She said she had already had several conversations with the leaders and that was the method by which she was attempting to gain consensus from them.

I guess you know by now that she was not successful in this effort. She made several critical mistakes. The largest of which was not taking the time to understand the true priorities of her peers in the leadership team of the corporation. Her objective was to drive through the concept of a new portal whether the company liked it or not. Her staff was very competitive, and I commended her for her competitive approach; however, she missed one crucial step and that was to understand the needs, the motives, and the goals of the company's leadership team and find a way to get them to work with her to achieve her goals. She was a "Lone Ranger." She was the one out there driving what she perceived to be the number one concern for the corporation and she was convinced that she could make it work in spite of the attitudes of the rest of the leadership team. I spoke with her for two or three months and then I got the phone call telling me she had just lost her job. I can understand why. "All I tried to do was work hard, be the best at my job, be competitive, and instill that competitive spirit in my team, yet it still wasn't enough for the leadership of the corporation," she said. She just didn't seem to understand that competing by yourself doesn't get you anywhere. You need to bring others on your team, and focus on the competition with your business competitors rather than internal competitions to promote your personal agenda. Being a Lone Ranger and competing only with yourself is a failure of leadership. The corporate world we live in today requires us to be influential team members rather than Lone Rangers.

> Being a Lone Ranger and competing only with yourself is a failure of leadership. The corporate world we live in today requires us to be influential team members rather than Lone Rangers.

Understand the Uniqueness of the Environment

Every company, industry, association, and affiliation has a unique culture and political environment. In order to be a successful leader, it is imperative that you take the time to understand the nuances of the organizations with which you are involved. Just look around you and you will find people who are well-liked and get things done because they understand their interactions with the team and the organization. Try to develop an understanding of their pattern of behavior in achieving these goals. This is just like competition, sizing them up and understanding why they are better than you are and where they may have weaknesses you do not share. Developing this understanding allows you to think honestly about your performance and make yourself a more formidable competitor.

Becoming a politically astute competitor is a challenge all leaders share. Doing so gives you the capability to excel in all

113

situations. Gaining an understanding of the competition gives you the ability to modify your behaviors and your approaches such that you can gain their support rather than their disdain, which leads to success. All too many of us feel this is manipulation, that through politics and networking we are really manipulating the behavior of others. It may be correct that our goal is to change the behavior of those around us, but doing so is the only way to reconcile the different backgrounds and experiences each of us brings to bear, which is a necessary step to becoming a successful leader.

To be an effective leader and build an effective team, you must include politics as part of the equation. As stressed more than once in this chapter, we all bring different backgrounds and points of view to a position. In order to build a cohesive team, it is important that we not only learn from each other but draw on each other's experiences and backgrounds to help make the best decisions possible. This is politics as I understand it; it is all about bringing together people from different perspectives and achieving a desired result.

We now live in a world where as leaders we can no longer mandate what we want done; we need to persuade people that our ideas are correct. To successfully persuade means learning to influence others, which requires us to approach others politically. This can be difficult to hear, but it really is the case in today's world. Being political doesn't mean standing up and giving speeches and running for office; it means monitoring the priorities and prejudices we all have as individuals and finding the common ground to be successful through persuasion rather than mandates.

Young people coming into the marketplace today have a different perspective on corporate culture and corporate ideals than those of us who have been working in a corporate environment for many years. The quality of life, the quality of the experience, the quality of their ability to compete, is all an

integral part of today's new generation. They are not as influenced by authority as prior generations were, and they are not
as close to the company culture as employees were in the past.
They are more doubting, more concerned with self-fulfillment,
and less invested in the corporation. I'm not saying these are
negative traits because, in a lot of ways, I think they are actually
positive. The next generation has finally figured out that it is
not about career first and life second. They feel that life is much
more important than career and that developing a successful career helps them to be better fulfilled in their individual lives. The
political challenge we face as leaders is how we balance their
needs and expectations with those of the older generations of
employees working within our organizations. This again comes
back to politics. Learning ways to influence the behaviors of
employees from every generation to achieve a common goal is
a critical aspect of becoming a successful leader today.

Each of us has a different level of competitive behavior, but
each of us has the potential to harness this competitiveness into
the controlled aggression necessary to succeed. Each one of
us has an inherent desire to compete—whether we recognize
it or not. Life is a competition, and we compete in various
ways every day. Competition is a good thing—something that
we should embrace rather than resist. Competition is the basic
driver of our success. It is not to say that we all have to be
overtly competitive. Rather, we should admit to ourselves that
it is an essential part of our being and not to be suppressed,
but aggressively controlled to adopt to the situation. It is one
of our basic instincts. Having the ability to compete also helps
us reduce stress. It is that relief valve that gives us the ability to
deal with frustration and day-to-day stresses. Humans have been
competing since the beginning of time. We used to compete for
food and tribal leadership. The Olympics have been around for
generations. Whether we like it or not, we all have an inert
desire to compete. It can be linked to our survival instincts. We

compete to survive and we compete to excel. We can't ignore our basic instincts and we also need to recognize that everyone has them. I am reminded of the phrase "To the victor go the spoils." There is another saying in racing: "Nobody remembers who finished second." I am not saying we all must be aggressive competitors, but we all need to recognize that competition is part of our human nature. Embrace it rather than denying it.

The message here is that competition is a positive influence in your daily life. Embrace your competitive impulses and use them as part of your decision-making process and as an element in your interactions with others. Competing isn't always about winning or losing; competing is really about learning to actively apply your skills, knowledge, and ability to influence the behavior of those around you and achieve a desired outcome. Sometimes that means compromise. A good competitor is one who understands the difference between winning the battle and losing the war. Understand those situations where it is okay to walk away, but learn from every one of those experiences in order to make yourself better prepared for the next competition.

> A good competitor is one who understands the difference between winning the battle and losing the war.

Competition breeds healthy tension in organizations. Without it they can get complacent. Some tension is a good thing. It keeps people on their toes and serves as a motivational tool. I can remember sitting around the board room and listening to my peers debating issues. In many cases there was disagreement. Our CEO would simply sit and listen to the debate. He would only get involved if it the rest of the team was at an impasse. He would then offer a suggestion to get the debate started again. In the end, we would always come to a mutually beneficial decision. He used to call this "healthy tension."

Having observed this process and been a part of it for many years, I gained a tremendous amount of respect for our CEO. Allowing us to compete with each other and reach a compromise made us a much stronger team. It wasn't about who won or lost, but learning to function as a team so we could all win.

No one ever wins every race, but we should strive to learn something from each one. We learn how to understand the behavior of others, we learn how to understand ourselves, and we learn to understand the limitations with which we are presented. We take those lessons and apply them to future situations in a process of constant improvement.

Competition is an individual thing. The degree to which we compete is part of our personal motivations. Don't be afraid to assess your strengths and weaknesses and find areas where you need to improve as you expand the comfort zone in which you enjoy competing. You don't need to be an overly aggressive competitor in every situation to win. The most successful people I know have a clear understanding of their comfort with competition in different environments. This is what it takes to excel as a leader. Know your strengths and limitations, know the areas in which you can succeed, and know the areas in which you can't. That is not to say that you can't be constantly trying to improve, but while you improve, play to your strengths and try to minimize the effects of your weaknesses. The most formidable competitors I have met through the years are the ones who beat me subtly rather than overtly.

CHAPTER 7

Do You Have Enough Friends?

Like most technologists, I spent the first part of my career focusing on the job at hand. My main objective was to do the best job I possibly could, accomplish the tasks assigned to me, provide the company with the best value, and fulfill my own individual drives and goals. Most technologists feel that way. We view the hard skills as the important things in our career because we can measure them and the value they provide the corporation. The problem is those are not the things that make you successful in the long run. Yes they get you started, they help you gain a reputation, and they give you personal satisfaction, but in the end, it is not really your hard skills that help you move up the corporate ladder.

I have been teaching college for many years now and the subject of my college discussion is "preparing for corporate life." When we enter the corporate world, most of us have no idea of the intricacies involved in succeeding within that environment. I always tell my students that when you begin your corporate life it is all about what you deliver rather than how you are perceived. This pendulum swings as you move up the corporate ladder. The higher you go in corporate life the more it is about how you are perceived than what you actually deliver. That is because the higher you go in corporate life it is more about relationships and the personal interactions between you and your peers, subordinates, and customers. As technologists, we are slow to understand this phenomenon. Most of us have similar personality traits, we tend to be introverts, we tend to like working alone, we tend to be very analytical in our thinking, and in a lot of cases we don't see the value in building strong personal relationships. To succeed in a corporate leadership position, you need to overcome these impulses and focus on building relationships.

For most of my career, it was normal to think of my friends as people with whom I interacted outside the workplace. My coworkers were considered purely professional acquaintances. I've mentioned before that we were trained through the early part of my professional career to be two people. It is important to reemphasize here that this type of separation of personal and professional lives can be detrimental to personal success and satisfaction. The key to success today is to be one person in all situations and create relationships wherever you interact with people inside or outside the workplace. At the end of the day, we're all just human beings and we all want to be treated fairly and to build relationships with others. Young people entering the workplace today come out of college with a new set of expectations. They look at a job as just part of a life in which the most important thing is their personal journey. I watch young people come into the corporate world and immediately begin building strong personal relationships with their peers. This was not the case many years ago, and I'm glad to see that we have overcome that stigma and are now looking at the workplace as another place to expand our relationships. I can't tell you how important it is for us as leaders to take on this posture as well. We need to understand that being a leader means being a relationship builder, being someone who is constantly looking to make new friends, build new relationships, and gain from those relationships.

> We need to understand that being a leader means being a relationship builder, being someone who is constantly looking to make new friends, build new relationships, and gain from those relationships.

You Need Friends to Succeed

I learned early on in my racing career that having friends is an essential element of success. When I first started out I was out for myself and only for myself and I viewed everyone else on the track as enemies I was bound and determined to defeat. I soon learned that in cars that are technically equivalent supported by teams that are equally prepared, winning is not just about your ability to take on the competition, it is about your ability to find friends out there so you can help each other. You see this a lot in NASCAR races where large tracts of drivers spend time drafting and pushing one another and helping each other along. Successful racing is all about teamwork. It took me quite a while to learn that lesson, and I still see that many of the young drivers today need to learn this lesson as they begin their racing careers. It is all about teamwork, making friends, and building a reputation as a team player and a fair person. Just like in corporate life, people like to team up with people they like. Without the help of others, I would never have been able to excel at racing.

When I first started my racing career, there was a driver on the circuit who was a multiple-time national champion. No one could compete with him as his skills far exceeded those of the rest of us in the group. One day during the early part of my career we were racing at the New Hampshire Motor Speedway. Since I was beginning my career, I was running by myself at the back of the pack trying to learn the craft and improve my technique. During this race, this exceptional driver came by me as the race leader. As usual, he was significantly ahead of every other competitor in the group. Suddenly he pulled in front of me and I started to follow and stayed with him for the next few laps. Then, just as suddenly, he left. It wasn't until the end of the race that I realized he was actually trying to help me by coaching me during the middle of a race. He knew I was new to racing and he was trying to use that opportunity to give me the chance to hook up with him so he could teach me the fast way around the track. I realize now that is exactly what he was doing; he was showing me where to turn, where to break, and when to accelerate. To this day I still remember that about him. Since that race, we have become very good friends, and we have raced competitively for many years. Although I've never beaten him, I will always remember that day when he took the time to help me in an unselfish manner. That is what relationships and building a network of friends is all about.

Early on in our careers it is very easy to advance to the next level of responsibility. It is easy because at that point in your career it is really based on your individual performance and the tangible benefits your work delivers to the business. There really is no need to have friends at that point, so you start out as an individual performer. In many ways, you are an unknown quantity at this point in your career. No one knows what type of team member you will be, and you don't have a personal history with others at the company that helps them understand how you will fit into the culture. Yes, we share ideas with others and we help out whenever we can, but it is basically individual performance that allows you to advance at that level because you have had so little opportunity to demonstrate your softer skills.

As we move up the corporate ladder into the management ranks, that model no longer works. Today's world is all about collaboration and working with teams in multiple locations. As you move up the ladder, your individual performance is increasingly overshadowed by your interactions with the team. It becomes imperative that you reach out and build friendships and relationships with the entire team in order to be successful. There are very few instances in today's world where people are able to advance without having built strong relationships with fellow team members. In some ways the new environment is moving closer to an educational model. For years, the corporate model and the educational model were totally different and this caused a lot of uneasiness for young people coming from colleges into corporations. Colleges emphasized teamwork for many years. In the last decade or so, corporations are finally starting to understand this and have begun to embrace a team environment. The Internet and other collaborative communication tools have allowed corporations to expand their teams beyond their physical walls and into the virtual world. This new environment is an even larger challenge as you try to build relationships with team members. No longer do we have the opportunity to walk down the hall and knock on the door or step out to lunch with someone. Now we need to understand how we can build strong relationships and friendships with team members who may be located across the country or around the world. It is imperative to become a strong communicator in order to survive in this new environment. As we develop ourselves as leaders it is important that we understand the need to begin building relationships and making friends at all levels as early in our careers as possible; communication is central to these efforts. Young people entering the workplace today understand and immediately begin this process. Older generations have not been as diligent about it and need to improve dramatically if they hope to become the trusted business partners they expect to be.

> Now we need to understand how we can build strong relationships and friendships with team members who may be located across the country or around the world.

Building a Network Is Critical

The higher we go on the corporate ladder the more we rely on our friends, our networks, and our relationships. These are the critical factors that determine success when you reach the management ranks. Below this level, jobs and their responsibilities are more rigidly defined with quantifiable results. This is not true at the management level. There is no right way or wrong way to lead, nor is there a single defined path to leadership. As you move higher up the corporate ladder, subjective measures become much more important than objective measures when evaluating your performance.

At the point in your career where you break into a leadership or management role, it becomes imperative that you consider building a strong network if you have not already begun to do so. The best leaders are the ones who use their network of contacts to address the gaps between personal strengths and weaknesses. This is a major shift in the way we behave and think about our jobs. It is no longer about us as an individual but rather about how we can leverage our network of business relationships and friends to help us grow and make better decisions. It is also about learning how to become a good collaborator rather than an individual contributor.

The first thing to do as you make this transition is to perform a self-evaluation. The problem with business structures today is that they require everyone to aspire to a leadership position in order to gain both personal and financial recognition. This should not be the case. Not everyone is cut out for a leadership position; not everyone desires a leadership role. I firmly believe that is why many of today's leaders are struggling with their performance and their reputations. Many of them are there because they have to be, not because they want to be. Compensation packages require us to move into management in order to continue to grow and to reach a higher pay grade. What smart companies should be doing is creating parallel paths for those who are less interested in being leaders than they are in developing the technical skills to make excellent individual contributions. We should not penalize some of our brightest people by forcing them to accept responsibilities they are ill-suited to perform. This type of environment forces people into situations where they are unable to leverage their real talents. In these cases the company loses. Leadership is not only about leading teams; it can also be about making high-quality individual contributions that employ your skills to ensure the success of the team. Becoming an effective leader means being able to modify your behavior and personality in some cases. This is not something to be taken lightly. I would strongly recommend that you consult a mentor as you work on this transition.

> The problem with business structures today is that they require everyone to aspire to a leadership position in order to gain both personal and financial recognition. Not everyone is cut out for a leadership position; not everyone desires a leadership role.

This transition to management causes most people with technical backgrounds much difficulty. Not all of us are able to make the transition successfully. The fact that many of us are introverts by nature makes the transition from a task worker to a leader much more difficult for technical workers than for more extroverted workers from other parts of the business such as sales or finance. If you are used to working alone more than seeking the advice of others, you need to make a behavioral change very early in your leadership career in order to become successful. You need to become more collaborative in your day-to-day work and you need to become more outgoing and social.

No Man Is an Island

Over the years, I have talked to many leaders and tried to convince them to network with their peers by joining organizations, attending events, and getting out of their office. I get the same answers all the time: "I'm just too busy." "I have too much on my plate." "I can't make the time to be able to do these things." The next call I usually get from them is that they lost their job, they don't know where to go, they have no network of friends, and they don't even have a resume prepared. In most cases, they panic and spend too much of their time criticizing the company from which they came rather than understanding that their demise was mostly due to their own performance. Had they built the network of strong relationships and strong friends a successful leader needs, they would be in a completely different situation. People whose mode of operation is to work hard, keep their heads down, and not worry about the softer aspects of the job tend to build a moat around themselves and become isolated from the rest of the corporation. The statement "No man is an island" comes to mind. Most of the senior executive recruiters I work with across the country tell me that a vast majority of leaders still do not understand the need to collaborate and build a network to help them in their careers.

I learned this lesson fairly early in my career. I had just landed a great job with a high-growth technology company after being recruited by one of the top search firms and going through an exhaustive evaluation process. Prior to accepting the position I had held a director of IT job at a somewhat smaller company with a very easygoing culture. I had a great relationship with my boss and all of the other leaders within the corporation. I really didn't spend a lot of time building those relationships; they just grew naturally without much work. I do think about the fact that outside my company I had a very sparse network of industry contacts.

My next position was with a much different company: It was a high-growth company with high energy and an extreme amount of competition at the management level. The first mistake I made was not to fully understand the culture I was getting myself into and the requirements for success in that culture. I thought just doing the right job and getting things accomplished would be enough, but it wasn't. I was naïve, like a lot of us are when we move up the ladder to positions at larger companies. I thought that as long as I worked hard and did a good job everything else would align. For the first two years, the company was performing very well; we were the fastest growing of our kind in our marketplace and things seemed to be running fairly smoothly. Most of the other top-level executives had strong ties and personal relationships, but I chose not to pursue personal relationships. I was always at work putting in long hours trying to accomplish the job at hand and I really didn't want to dedicate even more of my time to work so I could socialize with my peers. I also did very little socializing outside work. I joined industry organizations, but I didn't attend a lot of events. I just stayed at the office and worked as hard as I could to accomplish the goals of the corporation. I guess you know the rest of the story. One day while I was in my office the head of human resources called me to his office and told me someone had been recruited as my replacement and he wanted to talk to me about a severance package. I was devastated, scared, and emotional.

This was the first time in my life this had ever happened to me. I was always the one on the fast track getting the bigger job or recognition for a job well done. Now all that was over: I was getting fired.

The company assigned me to an outsourcing firm where they assisted me with the preparation of my resume. They gave me an office to work out of and helped me in my job search. I felt out of place. I was used to coming to an office every day to work and this was totally different. That was the first thing to hit me. The next thing was when they asked me to make a list of all the people I knew whom I could call. We sat down for two or three days and I found out my list of contacts was very short. Being an introverted technologist, I also had a difficult time getting on the phone and calling people to network because I felt inadequate now that I was out of work. Establish your network of contacts while you're employed because it is very difficult to build a network from scratch when you're not. I've spoken to many others in the same situation and they feel exactly the same way.

> Establish your network of contacts while you're employed because it is very difficult to build a network from scratch when you're not.

It took me several months to find my next position. It wasn't easy. I joined the local Society for Information Management organization, I attended as many of their events as I could in the area, and I learned that the only way to find a new job was to call people and write letters. I remember sitting there saying to myself "This will never happen to me again." During that transition time, I set goals for how many new people I would talk to each day and how many appointments I would set on a weekly basis. Once I was able to obtain employment again, I continued to set goals for myself. Every day I made it a point to talk to someone new, to reach out to someone I haven't spoken to before, to open dialogues with other members of the corporation. The lesson I learned from that experience was that you can never know enough people. To this day, I try to reach out and meet and connect with as many new people as I can. You never know where your next opportunity is going to come from, and you never know what is out in the marketplace unless you have a strong network.

Building a Network

Building a network is a task that needs to be a part of your daily activities. I remember when I was running my last organization I used to tell everyone in my department I expected them to talk to someone from outside our department every day. I did this for a couple of reasons. First, because I had learned firsthand the need to build a strong network; second, because it is important that people start to build strong bonds and relationships with their peers. I learned through the years that there were several activities that helped me as I built my network.

Building a new network is like acquiring friends. You have to be more of a friend to have friends. What I mean by that is you can't be selfish; you need to be open; you need to be more aggressive and more assertive in building the relationship. You should always be the one who reaches out. I have talked about this before; however, I feel that it is important enough to reiterate the need to build strong relationships. This is not to say that people will not reciprocate, but you have to be willing to be more aggressive in order to build and maintain a network. People have very short memories, so it is important to maintain this aggressive stance and reach out to your network on a regular basis. We have all heard the expression "out of sight, out of mind," and it is true of the people in our personal networks. Sometimes you have to find reasons to communicate with the people in your network. I found the easiest way to do this was to frequently update people on my personal status and ask them whether there is anything I can do to help them. It is important that you try to create this two-way communication in order to maintain a healthy and active network. Don't let too much time go by without contacting the members of your network.

> Don't let too much time go by without contacting the members of your network.

Throughout my career, we have relocated several times. When you move to a new area, the first thing you do is make new relationships and friendships with those living around you and with your coworkers. When you move away, there is a transitional period as you grow apart from those with whom you had strong bonds when you lived and worked together. We all start out with regular communications back and forth, but as we get caught up in our new day-to-day lives and our new environments we tend to communicate less with those we have left behind. Before we realize it, we no longer communicate at all and we have moved on. It is a sad fact that throughout our lives we will be able to make a certain number of strong relationships; you need to nurture those and keep them healthy and active as long as you possibly can. I make it a point at least once a month to go through my entire contact file and try to identify anyone I have not contacted in a while. I usually reach out to them with an update as to what is going on in my life and ask them to tell me what is going on in theirs. Most of the responses are quick and comprehensive. It just takes a little bit of time to reach out and maintain a good healthy network. Make sure you regularly allocate time to doing so.

Most of the opportunities throughout my career have come from my network. The good jobs hardly ever get advertised; they are passed through personal networks. This becomes more and more the case as we move up the corporate ladder. The best jobs in larger corporations are the ones that are filled through referral. If you don't have a strong network and a good reputation in the marketplace these opportunities will never come your way. I can't stress enough the need to continually build and nurture your personal network. I have a personal goal to add three to five new people to my network every week. You need to set a similar goal for yourself; otherwise, you are likely to ignore tending your network when faced with the pressures of daily life.

The older you get the more important your network is.

The older you get, the more important your network is. As we move into the twilight years of our career, reality sets in. Whether we like to believe it or not, age becomes a factor in our ability to acquire new opportunities. Most corporations are looking for people to fill new roles who can demonstrate the ability to grow and remain with the company for a period of time. They are making large investments in new executives and want to make sure they have filled a vacancy with someone who is able to deliver a strong return on that investment for years to come. The older we get, the fewer the opportunities like this will come our way. Many of us find our only options are to move into consulting or education. Both of these options require a strong network in order to succeed. If you have done your job right and built a strong network, leveraged that network to gain a good reputation in the marketplace, and nurtured those relationships, you will have built the foundation for a future as a consultant or educator. The good thing about those roles is we can perform them as long as we want. An even better thing is they provide us the opportunity to give back to those who are coming along based on our experiences. Not only are they financially rewarding, but these types of careers offer huge personal rewards. The way you are successful at this point in your career is through your reputation and you relationships, so don't take them lightly.

Always Be Willing to Help

I learned early on that when you're building a network you must always be willing to help members of your network by answering questions, providing assistance, or taking phone calls. People need to feel that you care about them and that they can come to you for guidance, help, or support. That is what building a strong network is all about. It is not about having expectations of them reciprocating, it is about wanting to help others in any way you can. The rewards will always be there, but you must earn them. Countless times I've helped someone in my network and many years later received an opportunity only to discover it was referred to me by the person I had helped so long ago. As I said, you should not help someone with the expectation of something in return, but spending the time to maintain a healthy network will lead naturally to opportunities.

One of the things I've always loved to do is putting together people from my network. I find people of similar interests or from similar industries and try to help them connect. You'd be surprised how rewarding this is, not only because you are able to help someone out, but because the people you help are thankful you took the time to remember them. Unselfish acts like these help you continue to build a strong network. Your reputation is an important element of your network, and by doing these things as you expand your network, you develop a strong reputation as a reliable and helpful colleague. Don't be selfish; don't always expect something in return. Your goal is to develop a reputation as someone who reaches out and helps others rather than someone always looking for payback.

> Don't be selfish; don't always expect something in return. Your goal is to develop a reputation as someone who reaches out and helps others rather than someone always looking for payback.

I can remember one example of a man I helped as a reference for three different jobs. Each time he was able to gain a new position thanks in part to the reference I provided him. During those three jobs, I started my own business, and I would talk to him about my company and what we were doing and ask his opinion. He was always willing to give an opinion; however, he was never willing to let my company interact with him. In addition, he would conduct business with competitors. The reason that I mention this is that I never really confronted him with this; however, when asked in the future for references I was not as forthcoming as I was in the past. It was not that I was expecting anything from him for helping out, but his actions told me the kind of person he was. He was someone who exploited those in his network rather than helping them and nurturing relationships. We have to be careful as we are building our networks that we take the time to understand the motivations of our friends and contacts. We need to make sure that we're not too closely tied to people who have reputations as being users rather than givers. This type of behavior can sometimes hurt you even though it is not the way you behave. So as you build your network, be careful whom you let in and understand their motives and behaviors so they do not reflect negatively on you.

I try to keep a record for everyone in my network with as much personal information as I can garner from them. As I always point out in the speeches I give around the country, the Internet has contributed to the rise of two social phenomena: instant gratification and personalization. We live in a society where we are impatient and want everything now. We also want to be treated as individuals. I have changed the way I create my network to address these new expectations through frequent contact and maintaining personal information about my contacts. You would be surprised to find out how well someone responds to you when you make that extra effort to know a little bit more about him or her as an individual. Sometimes it is sending a quick note about a sports team; other times it is making a call when you hear relevant industry news. These personal touches give you the ability to create a solid support network.

It Is All about Relationships

Building a strong network and building strong relationships through that network are the keys to success as a leader. I give many speeches around the country talking about leadership and leadership challenges. I tell each group I talk to that if they only remember one thing from what I've said they should remember the word "relationships." Relationships get us through life, both inside our corporations and in our personal lives. People only work with and socialize with people they like. The way to become liked is to build strong personal relationships. This is where it becomes difficult for those of us who have grown up as introverts. This is probably the most critical transition from a behavioral perspective that people need to make to become successful leaders.

Don't take this too lightly. Relationships lead to success. I've stated before that in today's world being able to work with younger coworkers is imperative to success. In order to become a trusted business partner and leader you need to take these bonds beyond just working together and develop strong personal relationships and friendships. At my last corporate job we had a team of 12 of us who were the operating committee of the company. We all came together as a team of friends over the years I worked at that corporation. We found mutual interests and looked for opportunities where we could share them outside the workplace. One in particular was racing. Most of us had an affinity for cars and enjoyed racing. Whenever we were away at a corporate meeting, we would always find the opportunity to either rent some go-karts or sign up for racing school so we could all get together and share our passion. This type of experience builds the bonds for future relationships. It is not just about the corporation that you are working with, either. The best opportunities I have had arose when a peer from my network moved on to a bigger and better position and asked me to follow. So build on these relationships, create friendships from them, and nurture them and you will be successful.

> In order to become a trusted business partner and leader you need to take these bonds beyond just working together and develop strong personal relationships and friendships.

The importance of building relationships was discussed in Chapter 5, but it feels important to bring the subject up again as relationships are the most critical path to success as an effective leader. It really also is tied to building a strong network. A network is not about having a Rolodex full of names—it is about having an individual relationship with as many people as you can.

> A network is not about having a Rolodex full of names—it is about having an individual relationship with as many people as you can.

Networks Are Connected

My talk about building networks and strong relationships isn't just about those people who are related to your career. A strong network extends to acquaintances outside the job. Just as you can't be two people, you can't maintain two networks, one for business contacts and one for personal contacts. When you think about integrating the aspects of your life, you find that we relate to people inside and outside work in the same ways. For many years, corporations have talked about building strong business relationships, but this is not a realistic approach. We need to develop a personal style that works for us no matter what the situation. As you build your network, consider it as one consolidated group of friends, acquaintances, and relationships rather than separate groups of business relationships and personal relationships. You would be surprised how many opportunities will come your way from connections that have no relevance to your current job or company. People get to know you and understand you over time, and information about you starts to circulate through their networks. After you have built these bonds, when someone hears about opportunities through his or her networks that are relevant to your background, you may find yourself connected with someone you wouldn't otherwise have met. That is why it is important to consider your network as one cohesive web, and also why it is important to never stop building out your network.

> As you build your network, consider it as one consolidated group of friends, acquaintances, and relationships rather than separate groups of business relationships and personal relationships.

LinkedIn (www.linkedin.com) is a very good example of my point. If you look at the numbers they quote, your network of

300 connections in turn connects you to 300,000 people. Each person you bring into your personal network has a separate personal network. As you multiply this over hundreds and hundreds of people, you begin to see how you can build a very effective and cohesive network. So, don't sit back and wait for people to come to you: Be aggressive about actively building your network.

Remember you can never have enough friends in this world. Relationships, friendships, and a strong network get us through the challenges of life. You never know when you may need to call on your network. I will give you a closing example. My wife was experiencing a medical problem and we were extremely concerned and didn't know where to turn. When we moved to our new community the first thing we did was to make as many friends as possible to help us integrate ourselves into the community. A few of those friends were doctors. I contacted one of my friends who is a doctor and explained my wife's situation to him. His first reaction was "Let me think about it and I will give you a call back." Within 20 minutes, he called back and had the name of what he felt was the best local physician to address her problem. He referred us to the other doctor and my wife was able to visit him and he treated her and we were able to successfully resolve the medical problem. It is just like in corporate life when you're dealing with someone you know personally or someone who knows a friend of yours personally, there is a different level of attention and a different level of concern. I know that all doctors are sworn by the Hippocratic Oath to provide the best care they can, but just as I said earlier in this chapter, human nature always contributes to our actions. People like to take care of those closest to them and those with whom they have built relationships. This was an excellent example of how building a strong network and having good relationships can pay off not just in the workplace but in every part of your life.

CHAPTER 8

What Is Your Balance?

L ife is such a short journey and the older that I get the more I realize how quickly it goes by. I look back over my career of over 40 years and some of it is a blur; it seems like much of it has sped by at warp speed. You remember things in general rather than specific terms until something happens that reminds you of a specific instance in the past. It is the same with my children. They are all grown now and have children of their own. Sometimes you forget the small quirks they had when they were children and suddenly you'll be watching a commercial or TV show and see a child do something that immediately triggers a memory of your own children. When I coach younger people, I always tell them to enjoy the journey and the time they have with their families. Many of them look at me rather strangely when they hear this advice because they don't understand how short life is. That is probably one of the hardest lessons I've learned, so I try to help people understand how quick the journey is and how it accelerates the older you are.

In corporate life, it seems we are always planning the next meeting, the next event, and the next trip. We are always thinking a week, a month, or two months out. Earlier in my career, I sometimes had a hard time remembering what month it was. I'd have to stop and say "This is January" or "This is July." I didn't recognize how crazy it was that I was so caught up in the activities of the job. I would say many of you have had the same experience. When days turn into weeks, weeks turn into months, and before you know it another year has passed.

Striving and Never Arriving

Very few of us tend to live in the moment. We are always living for the next experience or the next event. It took me well over 20 years in my career to start thinking about this and realize how quickly life was going by and how meaningless each day was becoming. About that time, I asked myself whether I was spending as much time with my family as I was on myself. It seemed as though my life was just about getting from one day to another. I have a friend who once used the phrase "striving and never arriving." I've always remembered it, and one of the turning points in my career came when I realized I need to make sure that every day makes a difference. I resolved to start making every day unique and to start thinking of my life from a position of balance. It reminds me of the greyhounds at the dog track continually chasing the mechanical rabbit. It seems as though in today's world we never reach fulfillment, all we seem to do is continue to chase the rabbit. The older and more experienced we get, the more we realize the value of fulfillment. We start our careers being very aggressive and always looking for the next challenge, the next hurdle, and the next opportunity. As we move through our careers and scale the corporate ladder, we tend to find more joy in the things we actually accomplish. I sometimes wish I had learned this lesson when I was much younger. I learned the hard way that most of the things I worried about and the outcomes I dreaded never happened. I was constantly concerned about the outcomes of actions over which I had no control. When you are caught up in this whirlwind of constantly striving and worrying about the outcomes of the next opportunity, life passes you by very quickly. Some of this is the aggression and impatience of youth;

140

however, some of it is also a part of our internal being. As I said, I only wish I had recognized that at an earlier point in my career. Reflecting back over my career it becomes obvious to me that 90 percent of the things that I worried and planned for never happened and, of the other 10 percent, less than 5 percent actually happened or occurred the way I perceived them. It makes me angry that I spent a large part of my life worrying and striving for outcomes over which I had no control and which mostly never occurred.

> You need to focus on the things you have the best chance of controlling and worry less about those beyond your control.

You need to focus on the things you have the best chance of controlling and worry less about those beyond your control. This is not easy to do, especially for motivated people. I still get mad at myself when I get stressed about something that really doesn't matter. We all want to make sure that everything moves smoothly. What we need to realize is that we have a limited amount of time and need to focus on the important things first and worry about the rest later. Even understanding this, I often find it difficult separating the two types of concerns. My approach is to set goals and priorities at a macro level. This can be by the day or week. When you are hit with an issue, test it against the goals you have set. If it doesn't fit, push it down the list. I find that making a list is the best way for me to control my activities. I modify it each day based on changes in priorities. Having a list gives you the ability to focus and make sure things don't fall through the cracks. I have found that lists work for me in all settings, including racing. I think this is where I first started doing it. If you forget to tighten something before you go out, you are in trouble. We have a checklist that we go over each time the car comes off the track, so it was a small change for me to adapt this technique to my personal and business lives. We can't remember everything, so keeping a list helps. It is also a great way to set priorities. I always carry a piece of paper and a pen with me. Doing this reduces stress, allows me to focus on important issues, and ensures things don't slip past. The list provides a sense of confidence, and it allows you to feel calmer and more peaceful.

You need to learn to separate the things you should worry about and the situations you should strive to change from those over which you have no control. It is the journey and your enjoyment of it that matters. Becoming a trusted business partner requires you to adopt this approach. You need to take the time to listen, observe, and understand those issues you can influence and those you can't. You need to communicate these differences with your peers and work with them in a collaborative way to exploit the things you can influence and mitigate those you can't. You also need to make sure you have a mechanism to ensure you address the right priorities and don't lose track of others that need to be addressed later. It is much easier to lead effectively if you have reached that comfortable position in your life where you have control over yourself and the environment around you.

Make Every Day Unique

For many of us, our days are surprisingly similar. We tend to wake up every day at the same time, to follow the same schedule, and even to consume a lot of the same foods. Corporate life tends to cause us to become regimented in our activities and thoughts. You sometimes feel like a robot. It is easy to be consumed by corporate culture and live within an extremely structured environment. Maybe this is a throwback to the days of the assembly lines, I'm not sure, but in many cases the structured nature of today's corporate life makes it difficult to break

142

free and change each day unless you make a concerted effort to do so.

I once had a job in Chicago where I watched a group of people from my department every day at lunch. They were so regimented that after a couple of weeks, I could tell you what table they would sit at, what seat they would sit in, and pretty much what they would have for lunch. They had worked at the same company for many years, some of them for decades. After observing them for several weeks, I questioned them and they were aware of their repetitive behavior. While I was in Chicago, I took the train to work every morning. I learned that everyone on the train had a favorite seat when I sat in the "wrong one" the first week I began my commute. It wasn't long before I had my assigned seat on the train as well. I guess I fell into the mold just like everyone else. This can be dangerous as you can become complacent, which can adversely affect your life. Not to say that people who have repetitive jobs cannot be successful and enjoy life, but each of us should strive to take a portion of each day and make it unique. I really believe that taking the effort to create some uniqueness in our lives creates mental stimulation, which fosters creativity and causes us to be more observant. A good example of that would be to have several people walk the same route to work every day and ask each of them what they saw on the way to work on a particular day. The people who are trying to make a difference in each day will probably have much more detailed observations of what they saw on the walk than those who didn't. The people comfortable with repetition, who likely never even looked to either side, probably never noticed the activities around them.

Test this yourself some time. Drive down the street and instead of just focusing on the road ahead, take some time to glance from side to side. You will be surprised at what you might observe. You may see things about houses you never noticed before, you may observe animal behavior you have never seen before, and you may see some new things you never knew were there before. Do this on the street you live and take the time to make a mental note of all the new things you have observed. After a few trips down the street, you will find the trip becomes enjoyable rather than just a passage from one place to another. I'll say this many times throughout the chapter, but we are all on this earth for a limited period of time, and it is important that we all take the time to enjoy the journey, relish our experiences, and observe the world around us. It is amazing how much your perspective changes when you take the time to be observant. It makes the journey more pleasant and fosters deeper thought. You start to think about the nature of things more than you ever did before.

Being observant is extremely critical to being a leader. We get so caught up in ourselves that we don't take the time to observe the behaviors of others; we lose that trusted relationship and perspective we all seek as leaders. We need to take a step back and observe the behavior of others, the approach they take to their work, and their individual personality traits in order to become a more effective leader. You also find that by doing this you will gain a tremendous amount of respect from those around you. They will feel honored that you have taken the time to understand them and their personal needs, behaviors, and skills.

> Being observant is extremely critical to being a leader. We need to take a step back and observe the behavior of others, the approach they take to their work, and their individual personality traits in order to become a more effective leader.

I always make it a point to walk around the building and engage with as many people as I can. Doing this, you learn a lot about how different people behave and react to situations. The best way to learn is to ask questions. I start out asking people what they are working on and how it is going. Based on their response, I then probe more deeply. If someone says things are not going well, I ask what the trouble is. Continuing to probe gives you a good picture of a person's decision process and reaction to stress. After doing this for a while, you get better at seeing patterns without having to probe so deeply. This type of understanding is an important element when building relationships. When you understand key behavioral traits, you can use them as a guideline when you engage others. For example, if you know a certain person has an excitable nature, you do not want to hit him or her with a problem right away. Instead, find something that interests the person and open a conversation with it before working around to the challenge you want to discuss. You will find people are in a much more relaxed state of mind and more open to discussing a problem if you approach it slowly.

Sitting in a meeting with your peers is a great opportunity to learn more about their behavioral traits. This is a safe environment for you to observe them. I always watch the interactions of the group and after a while I can usually predict how each person will react to topics that arise. I make notes to myself about each one of them; their interests, what seems to motivate them, whether they are controlling, whether they open to suggestions, and so on. This is similar to how our children monitor our behavior and learn how to push the right buttons. We all remember which parent we could go to for what and how we influenced them. This process can work when building business relationships, and it will help you feel more confident in your interactions and allow you to keep your inner balance.

I'm using these examples to show you how programmed we become in our day-to-day lives and how regimented and repetitive our lives can be. My initial reaction is that this kind of behavior stifles creativity and stifles leadership. When nothing ever changes and we do the same thing day in and day out, it is very hard to be creative and collaborative. I'm sure this phenomenon is apparent in most of the corporations across our country.

This behavior became a catalyst for me to understand that I needed to change my life. Many years ago, I made a commitment to myself that I needed to change my outlook and be more flexible in my thoughts and observations. I made a commitment to make every day unique, not to fall into the rut of performing the same routines day-in and day-out. I started out by walking a different way to the office every day. At the time, I lived in Chicago and could walk from the train station to the office in approximately 20 minutes. I found myself taking the same streets every morning. After I convinced myself of the need to make every day unique, I would take a different route to work each day. It is not that I wouldn't repeat myself, because there are only so many streets, but that I made a conscious effort to start each day a little differently.

I remember one day I decided to take a longer route. It was a nice morning and I didn't have meetings right away, so I thought I would take a more roundabout path. As I was walking, a gentleman came up beside me and started walking beside me. He asked me if I was from Chicago. I told him I was actually from the Boston area and that I had recently moved to Chicago. I then asked him whether he was from Chicago and he said he was born and raised there and had spent his entire life in the city. The next thing I noticed as I was walking with him down the sidewalk and talking was how many people came by and said good morning. After maybe the third person I turned to him and asked if he was the mayor. He looked at me and laughed and said, "Yes, I am." You can only imagine how surprised I was to find myself walking on the sidewalk side by side with the mayor of Chicago without recognizing him. I then noticed after he identified himself that two rather large individuals were walking behind him and then understood fully that he was, in fact, was the mayor of Chicago. If I hadn't changed my route to work every day, and if I hadn't decided to make that journey special, I probably never would have met him.

Many months later my wife and I were at the dedication for a new library in Chicago and the mayor was there speaking. It was a rather large and well-attended event, and we had a wonderful evening. Following his speech, the mayor made the rounds of the room. When he spotted me and my wife in the corner, he came over to us, looked at me, and said, "You're the fellow from Boston I met on the sidewalk who didn't know who I was, aren't you?" I looked at him and laughed somewhat embarrassed and said, "Yes, that's me." We both laughed, my wife laughed as well, and he began to tell the audience around us the story of how we met. Here is a good example of a wonderful experience I had because I made every day unique. Like the saying goes, you never know.

Later I decided to use this approach everywhere and take a different route no matter where I was going. I would always try to find a new way to get to a meeting, an event, or anywhere else I had to go. This conditioned me to become more observant and also made life more exciting. Rather than reacting to a routine, I was acting each day and paying more attention to my senses, my emotions, and the world around me. I think that is why some of the most creative people I have known tend to be the happiest. I think of artists. People who spend days and weeks to get the right light and the right setting to create the painting they have in mind. I have a friend who is an artist and he tells me that he will visit hundreds of locations before he sees the one he wants to paint. After he finds the right location, he takes photographs throughout the day looking at the angles of the sun and clouds and environment around the image he wishes to paint. After taking several pictures over several weeks he then finds the ideal time and situation to capture. Before he has even put paint to canvas, he has spent weeks observing and preparing. When the process of painting begins, it becomes a combination of the reality of the scene and his own emotional observations of it, and it is the combination of these two things that enables him to create a masterful painting. I think he is probably one of the happiest people I know, and I truly believe that is because he takes the time to enjoy life and to revel in the beauty of the scenes in the world around him. Try it for yourself. Find someone who is creative, whether it is a painter or sculptor or other type of artist, and observe that person's behavior. I think you will be surprised to find that we can learn a lot through them and from them. What you see is that they are the type of people who do not immediately react to situations; instead, they take the time to think things through and formulate a plan before they begin. The best leaders I have known act this way as well. They do not have a knee-jerk reaction, but rather a more calculated and considered one.

To be an effective leader, we need to recognize that our immediate response to one day, one issue, or one situation does not change the course of our lives. However, choosing to take the time to appreciate the moment, assess the situation, and deal with it from a perspective of openness rather than a programmed reaction can. Building a strong trusting relationship with your peers is difficult; but if you adopt this approach to life, you will find that it becomes easier to gain their trust and to interact with them. You are not just taking the corporate line. The more you are observant and aware of the situation and your surroundings and using that information in your conversations and interactions with others, the more human and approachable you will be to others. People will find you refreshing and enjoyable. They will make time to talk to you and consult you. People's confidence in you will grow when they realize that you have a behavioral model they would like to achieve themselves. Use this to your advantage in building the strong trusting relationships that are the foundation of success.

I would challenge you to find ways to make every day unique. You will be pleasantly surprised to see how much more enjoyment you get out of every day. You will also be surprised to see how much more of each day you remember. Even more important, I hope you find as I did that being more observant helps you open your mind to new things and new challenges. Bottom line: Adopting this attitude will make you more successful in your job and your day-to-day life. It gives you the ability to look at things with a more open perspective rather than just based on prior experiences. In the business world, we need to constantly look for ways to improve. We all have individual backgrounds that can severely restrict creative and fresh thinking. Adopting an attitude of living more in the moment and slowing down to the pace of our lives gives us the clarity we need to be more creative. You will also find that it opens your mind to the possibilities around you and allows you to free yourself from the day-to-day structure and experience the essence of life. Just remember that the job experience is only one part of your life and make sure you put it in perspective as you enjoy the journey.

> Adopting an attitude of living more in the moment and slowing down to the pace of our lives gives us the clarity we need to be more creative.

Filter Your Input and Make the Right Decisions

The secret to being a successful racecar driver isn't always being the fastest one around the track. This might seem odd when you are in a sport built around fast cars, but the best racers are the

149

smoothest racers. They are the ones who understand the need to pace themselves, to enter the corner at the right speed such that they can hit the apex of the corner and be at full speed coming out the other end, hitting the right breaking points time and time again, and knowing where and when to shift. The other secret to maintaining as much speed as possible as you are going through the corners is to keep the car as loose as you possibly can. These are the things that allow you to be smooth and gain speed when racing. When you become proficient at this, it makes you a very formidable competitor. It is not about how fast you can enter the corner—it is about how fast you can exit it. If I break a little earlier but at the apex of the corner I am on the throttle two or three tenths of a second before you are, I will gain all of that momentum for the rest of the straightaway to the next turn. Racing is about gaining as much momentum as you possibly can with every movement you make. It is a combination of choreographed moves. The fastest racecar drivers I know make racing appear effortless. In my own experience, the fastest laps I have returned were the ones that felt somewhat slower but also felt smoother and more confident.

I raise this point because there is a speed and smoothness to life as well. The society we live in today, with all of its gadgets and tools, causes us to be in constant motion. We are continually bombarded by external stimuli whether it is our cell phone, our iPad, or any other electronic device. We also become used to multitasking. You no longer watch the news on TV, what you see is the newscaster in the center of the screen and streaming information above and below. This is also true in our daily lives at work. We are constantly required to multitask and we are constantly being bombarded with information. I'm not saying this is a bad thing, but I am suggesting it inhibits our ability to slow down and react to the speed of life. We seem to have lost our ability to just sit and focus on one thing. We can't go more than two minutes without checking our e-mail on our mobile devices or our desktop. We are in constant contact with everyone else in the world. I understand this is necessary in the business world today and that it can provide benefits; however, I disagree with the idea that it is the only way we can be successful in today's world. I still believe the best leaders and the most successful people are the ones who step back from this environment on a regular basis and spend time focusing on a specific task or just sitting and thinking creatively about something that may be important to them. There is a television commercial that shows young campers driving up a hill. The reason why is a mystery as they keep checking their cell phone. Then, all of a sudden, they get to a point where there is no cell service. Here they stop, celebrate, and pitch their tent having found where civilization ends and the wilderness begins. This is exactly what I mean: We all want to get away, we all get frustrated with having to be in constant communication, and we all need to take that time for ourselves.

> One of the tricks I have learned in my business career is to manage by exception.

One of the tricks I have learned in my business career is to manage by exception. Like everyone else, I was bombarded with information from multiple sources and constantly pulled in different directions. I learned through the years to sit back and try to assign a relevance weighting factor to each stimulus. This allows me to understand what I really don't need to be involved with, what I should continue doing, and what I am ignoring that requires my attention. I tell my direct reports I wouldn't need them if I had to be involved in every decision—that I hire brains not buttons. Each of us has a set of skills and an intellect we need to use as members of a team. If one person is involved in every decision and must oversee every bit of information flowing into an organization, the team can never be successful. You need to manage by exception. You will never read and comprehend all of the information that is available to you. What you need to understand is what things are important, and what pieces of information will help you become a more successful leader. Focus on this information and the gaps you have in your background and try to constantly gain knowledge to fill those gaps. Learn to understand when information that is coming your way is either irrelevant or something that should be handled by others. You must learn to prioritize what you do, what you need to react to, and what you need to hand off to someone else. This doesn't come easily and takes a lot of practice when faced with the large amount of information available to us today. However, if you observe successful leaders today you will see that it can be done. They have developed an ability to be selective in the things with which they are involved and the information they use as part of the day-to-day job.

> We need to reduce the amount of information we use to make decisions to a manageable level so we can react in a timely manner.

Being an effective leader means understanding the things that are important and the things that are not. It is about knowing how to pace yourself and build trust with others. The pace of decisions in today's world is becoming faster and faster. It is necessary for us to understand which issues are critical enough to influence our decision process and use those as the drivers for our decisions. We need to filter out the external factors and the noncritical issues. We need to reduce the amount of information we use to make decisions to a manageable level so we can react in a timely manner. We have all heard the term "analysis paralysis," and it is a major concern in today's world. Not only are decision windows becoming smaller, but the information available to us is expanding. As leaders we need to be able to synthesize, filter, and personalize that information into a manageable set of questions to help our decision process. This gets back to my earlier point of understanding our priorities, focusing on the information that is germane to them, and ignoring the rest of the information available to us. Don't just have business priorities, have personal development priorities as well. We are barraged with information today and cannot possibly process it all. I regularly place filters on the information sources I use when making decisions. I categorize my sources into business, personal improvement, and entertainment. The more you can categorize your sources and filter the content, the easier it is for you to process the information available to you. Try to allocate time for all sources, but be comfortable ignoring the ones that are not of immediate importance to the decision at hand. This exercise is critical to becoming an effective leader. It gives you the ability to create a balance of understanding business priorities while also keeping abreast of your specific professional advances. Time allocation and information prioritization is of paramount importance to effective leadership.

After you have control over the information coming in, you need to break decisions down into smaller pieces. There is an old adage that you "only eat an elephant one bite at a time." This is the way we make good decisions as well. Try to synthesize the information and categorize it into short term, medium term, and long term. The more you break a decision down into smaller, more measurable pieces, the easier it is for you to make that decision; more importantly, you then have several checkpoints along the way to reassure yourself that you have made the right decision. This gives you the means to monitor your decision over time. You can only do this by taking the time to filter through the barrage of information, to understand the ultimate objective, and to break it down into manageable pieces. The more you follow this process, the more success you will have, and the more trust you will build with your peers. That is not to say you won't make mistakes, but this approach provides the ability to react quickly when things go wrong and to make adjustments. This sounds like a difficult task, but it really isn't. All you need to do is tie your decisions to a particular set of tenets. Whether they are the tenets of the strategy of the company, the tenets of the architecture with which you are working, or the rules of engagement with your competitors. After you establish those tenets and quantify them, it becomes easy to reach decisions.

> The more you break a decision down into smaller more measurable pieces the easier it is for you to make that decision; more important, you then have several checkpoints along the way to reassure yourself that you have made the right decision.

Slow Down to the Pace of Life

In today's world we tend to operate at a high rate of speed whether it is on the racetrack or in the office. We fail to recognize that in many cases we are missing the essence of life. Even though we are living in a society where information is moving at a rapid rate—automobiles go faster, airplanes go faster, everything seems to be continually increasing in speed—we need to take a step back and understand the real pace of life. Even though we have increased the pace of technology and the pace of decisions, trees still grow at the same rate, flowers still grow at the same rate, and we grow as individuals at the same rate. This tells me the basic speed of life has not changed. What has changed is that the outside stimuli we receive from our jobs and the rest of the world has increased its pace. We have tried to adjust to this by moving faster, making decisions sooner, walking a little faster, and trying to speed up almost every part of our day. I'm not saying that we can ignore the fact that society is moving at a much faster rate than it ever has before, what I am saying is that we need to understand that even though society and the flow of information is moving more rapidly, the rest of our surroundings have not changed.

In many cases, we can become more successful if we slow ourselves down to the speed of our surroundings. This means as a leader that we need to take the time to breathe deeply, take a walk, or perform any activity that makes us feel comfortable and relaxed in order to regain a fresh perspective. In racing, we can only go fast for so long and then we run out of gas and wear down our tires. We need to make a pit stop to be refueled and have our tires replaced, but also to have a drink of water and prepare ourselves for the next set of challenges in the race. Life is like that as well. We need to take these times where we can slow down, refuel ourselves, and prepare for the challenges ahead. Too many executives feel the need to be constantly stimulated and never really take time for themselves. This causes them to burn out at an early age and affects their ability to interact with others and build the relationships and trust necessary for success. The best leaders I've known have been the ones who have understood this and modified their behavior to be more tuned to the process and the speed of life rather than constantly getting caught up in the whirlwind of society. It is difficult for us to make rational and effective decisions when our minds are not clear, we are not relaxed, and we haven't taken the time to do the proper analysis. It is funny that in racing, the most successful drivers I know are the ones with the most laid-back personalities. The ones who crash the most are the ones who are nervous and wound up all the time. I've also observed this behavior in the corporate world. The leaders who have been more relaxed and calculating have had more successes than the ones who were overly emotional.

> The leaders who have been more relaxed and calculating have had more successes than the ones who were overly emotional.

My daughter has two sons who couldn't be any more different. Gross is a high-energy and extremely nervous person. I watch him, his actions, and his decision processes. He tends to react extremely quickly and in most cases think about those reactions only after the fact. I feel that he has been shaped by our society and its overwhelming stimuli, and it has made him emphasize action over careful thought. My other grandson is exactly the opposite. I used to ask him questions and he wouldn't answer me for a while and I would get aggravated because I thought he was ignoring me. One day I asked a question, he didn't answer me, and I asked him again to please answer the question I had asked. He responded that he was thinking about his response. I stopped in my tracks and couldn't believe what I was hearing from this five-year-old. He decided that rather than react quickly he was going to take the time to process the question, analyze it, and come back with a calculated response. I believe that in life we need to adopt an approach balanced between those of my grandsons. We need to be responsive, assertive, and bold, but also calculating. It is this balance that allows us to become successful leaders and trusted partners.

> Remember that the most effective leaders have understood how to balance the pace of society and the pace of life.

156

Remember that the most effective leaders have understood how to balance the pace of society and the pace of life. It is understanding this balance and applying it to our day-to-day lives that give us the capability to make clear, calculated, and unemotional decisions. More importantly, it creates an environment where our peers and our team members feel comfortable interacting with us and they know that at the end of the day we have the ability to help them make better decisions.

CHAPTER 9

How Good Are You at Sales?

The interesting thing about racing is it is not just about your ability as a driver, it is also about your ability to sell yourself to sponsors. That is the thing that has bothered me most throughout my racing career. I've seen many good drivers leave the sport because of a lack of funding. The sport of racing is all about money, and you must gain sponsorship and support to succeed. The most successful drivers recognize this early on and adjust their personalities to become as much salespeople as drivers. I remember an extremely successful driver, who is now one of the top professionals in the world, telling me the difference between him and another friend of mine he raced early in his career was that he had the ability to sell himself and my friend did not. He told me professional racing is all about selling yourself to bring business to your sponsors. Drivers looking to go pro who didn't grow up rich need to understand this lesson and quickly begin selling themselves Young drivers never seem to realize this until they have a few years of experience and want to move to the next level. At that point, if they don't have family or other financial support, they realize they need to find a way to pay for their careers on their own. This is when you see the difference between those who have a passion for racing and those who do not. The young drivers who were successful in racing were able to develop that skill and sell themselves to potential sponsors: to convince people to believe in and support them. The smart ones also sought out those of us a few years older in search of experience and connections. They would spend time with us to learn the rules of engagement and what it takes to be successful in the world of corporate sponsorship. That is a world in which they need to play because that is where the money is. So when you look at a professional racing series and you see all of the successful drivers you now understand what it takes to achieve that level.

> The need to sell yourself is essential to success in corporate life as well. Ability alone will not get you to the leadership positions you hope to achieve.

The need to sell yourself is essential to success in corporate life as well. Ability alone will not get you to the leadership positions you hope to achieve. It is not that talent doesn't play a role in success, but pure talent isn't enough to give you the foundation you need to advance your career. As discussed in Chapter 7, this isn't a major problem when you are first starting out. Early in your career, you are judged primarily based on personal performance. You then reach a level where the most important criteria shift from personal performance to the success of teams you lead. That transition is slow at first as you move into the initial roles of leadership; however, it accelerates from there. We tend to trivialize the need to develop our personal sales styles as we begin our climb up the leadership ladder, but taking this need seriously can help you make the transition from roles requiring strong individual performance to those requiring success as a leader. The best way to start is to prepare as early as possible in your career. Many people I've known have joined outside organizations to help them build their sales style. Some that come to mind are Dale Carnegie courses, local college courses, or membership in community organizations. When I was young, I became very active in a group called the Jaycees. This was an organization designed for young men and women in the business world to help them advance their careers while providing service to their community. I truly believe that having that experience in my late 20s and early 30s helped me tremendously in building the foundation I needed as I moved into leadership roles.

My experience in the Jaycees was far more valuable than I ever could have imagined at the time. It helped me build skills I still use today as a corporate leader. We built strong personal relationships as members of the organization, worked closely together on community projects, and helped each other in our day-to-day lives. I had bought a new house at the time and was installing an in-ground pool in the backyard. I wanted to build a shed for the filter so we wouldn't have to listen to the sound of the filter running when we were in the pool. I mentioned to a few of my friends in the Jaycees that I was going to build a shed one weekend and lo and behold on Saturday morning six of them showed up to help me. This is the type of relationships you need to build in corporate life as well. Organizations like the Jaycees teach you how to build these relationships, how to nurture them, and how to work effectively with others to achieve shared goals. Another great program they had was a speakers program. We each competed on a local level then moved from there to state and from state to national. This program was unique because we were working with our peers and our friends as we were developing our speaking and presentation skills. This offered us the opportunity to work in a much less stressful environment where everyone in the audience was helping you be successful. I don't think you can buy that kind of experience; you need to seek it out through your personal relationships.

Presenting Is Entertaining

When I got too old to belong to the Jaycees, I moved on to industry associations and served on several boards within my community. These experiences helped me further develop my sales and presentation skills. I don't think we understand enough how important it is for us to become effective communicators and presenters as we try to build trust with others. Presenting in a professional manner is the most effective way to convey your message successfully to others. I speak around the country regularly about the topics of leadership and organizational development. I tell people that in these presentations, as well as those we give in corporate life, 80 percent of the presentation is about the subject matter and information you want to convey and 20 percent of the presentation is entertainment. If you don't use that 20 percent to entertain and invigorate your audience, your message will never be heard. I've sat through countless dry and boring presentations and on almost every occasion I failed to take away one nugget of information afterward. Think about your own experiences in meetings and presentations and you'll see what I mean. The most successful presentations are those in which the presenter has passion for what she or he is presenting, the materials are of value to the audience, and the presenter's delivery keeps the audience engaged with the subject matter.

We can all think of presenters who have failed to engage an audience. The ones who stand in front of a crowd, put slides up on the screen, and just stand there and read from the slides. It is almost insulting when you sit in the audience because the presenter seems to believe you are illiterate. The best presenters understand the audience is there to hear the presenter's ideas rather than to have a lesson in remedial slide reading. They tend to use very few slides, each one presenting only one or two essential pieces of information. The slides are nothing more than a roadmap for the presentation. They allow the presenter to direct the audience's attention to a handful of key points that form the heart of the presentation. It is not that these presenters fail to use slides to clarify and quantify their ideas, but they don't let the slides serve as the presentation. Audiences want to engage with human beings: You should be the one presenting information, not your slides.

> The best presenters understand the audience is there to hear the presenter's ideas rather than to have a lesson in remedial slide reading.

When I'm presenting, one of the most important things I do is watch my audience. I observe their attentiveness, body movement, and facial expressions. When you are presenting to a group, whether large or small, keep them interested and engaged so they aren't lost in the material you are trying to present. The most important thing when presenting to others is to make sure the message you want conveyed is clearly and forcefully presented to your audience. If you notice during your presentation that you are losing the audience's interest, you need to adjust your style. Sometimes that means changing the tone of your voice, other times it means engaging the audience more through strategies like active questioning. I particularly enjoy giving presentations in a workshop format. The audience is there to listen to my experience, but getting them engaged and making them part of the presentation provides a learning experience for all of us. At the start of every presentation, I tell

163

the audience the presentation is designed to be an interactive session and that I want them to be responsive and interactive so we can all learn together. I also tell them if I ask for questions and none come from the audience I will come down and start picking people to question. You will find that breaking the ice in this way encourages others to join in and engage in conversation. By using this technique, I usually achieve a lively interaction with the audience.

Most presentations follow a pattern of increasing comfort between presenter and audience. When it starts out there is a coldness and lack of interaction in the room. The best presenters are able to build a collaborative environment while they are presenting. Just think about it the next time you go to an all-day seminar. You all start out not knowing each other, trying to keep to yourself, and not being very engaging, but at the end of the day everyone is sitting back comfortably, conversation is flowing, and people are truly enjoying the experience. I've watched many meetings and presentations over the years and the best ones have had this sort of flow of engagement and interaction. Think about that as you prepare your presentation. As presenters it is our responsibility to build that collaborative environment through our presentation. The best way to do that is to practice your presentation skills and engagement strategies on people you know, like I did with the Jaycees.

Another trick I have learned through the years is whenever I'm giving a presentation or speech, I always try to have someone in the audience who is prepared to ask the first question when I open the floor for interaction with the audience. Having this seed question breaks the ice and offers you the opportunity to take that question, build on it, and ask more on that topic to further engage the audience. It almost always works. All it takes is that one person to break the ice and start the water flowing downstream.

Another trick I have learned through the years is whenever I'm giving a presentation or speech, I always try to have someone in the audience who is prepared to ask the first question when I open the floor for interaction with the audience.

The same techniques work whether we are talking to an audience of hundreds or just one person. In these situations, people are looking to us to create value, and we need to be able to deliver it in a way that builds their enthusiasm to hear more. Thinking about our education provides a good example of this. Think about the professors and teachers you liked best. You'll likely find that they were the ones who were the most entertaining and engaging. You learned because they were able to create a collaborative environment where you were comfortable and entertained, which opened you to new ideas. In order to be successful in corporate life, consciously strive to create that same environment. It is all about an ability to convey your message and have it accepted in the way in which you intend.

At the time of this writing, we are preparing for a presidential election. Some of us are happy this only happens once every four years. We are constantly hearing a barrage of campaign speeches. If you look back over time, the most successful candidates have typically been the best orators. They could connect with their audience and convey a message that resonated. It isn't always the speaker with the best ideas, or the most impressive background, who best convinces an audience, it is often who can foster a sense of connection with an audience. Politics, just like corporate life, is all about sales. It is selling yourself, your ideals, and your style. People tend to elect candidates with whom they feel they can connect on a personal level. Politicians have developed a unique knack to develop this sense of connection consistently with a range of different audiences. We all know they'll never deliver on everything they promise, but they are able to build that sense of personal connection with us and convince us to vote for them. Voting is a popularity contest, as is leadership in the corporate world. At the end of the day when we pull the lever, in most cases, we are voting for the person we like more as an individual, even more than the values the candidate stands for. This is a sad testimony about democratic society in general; however, it drives home the point that becoming an effective leader requires you to become an effective presenter who knows how to appeal to an audience and get them to feel a personal bond with you.

CEO Means Chief Sales Officer

When I took my first CEO job at *Computerworld* (http://www .computerworld.com/), I never realized that my real title was "chief sales officer" rather than "chief executive officer." Most of my time was spent visiting clients with sales representatives, helping out on sales calls, and focusing on developing revenue for the company. It seemed like almost all of my time was consumed with sales. That is not what I expected when I was appointed chief executive officer, but as the face of the company, you are expected to be a driving force creating revenue for the company.

Many of us in corporate life tend to try avoiding people involved in sales. I was guilty of that as well until I began to understand that without a sale nothing happens. The best leaders are the best salespeople. When you are running a company, it becomes obvious that strong sales are critically important to the success of your company.

While I was the CEO at *Computerworld*, I started to reflect on my career up to that point. At first I thought this was a unique environment that was more sales-oriented than business-oriented. But thinking back over my career in corporate life made me realize being CEO wasn't the first time I was asked to focus on sales. Previously, it was more about selling myself than selling products, but I spent every day selling my work, a concept, or a solution to a problem. Because IT is a support organization within the corporation, the only way to succeed is to gain the consensus of your peers. Doing so requires selling to your colleagues. Whether we like it or not, we are constantly promoting ourselves in our business and personal lives. I don't mean that in a derogatory way, but in a realistic way.

> Because IT is a support organization within the corporation, the only way to succeed is to gain the consensus of your peers. Doing so requires selling to your colleagues.

I started my own company 10 years ago. My primary concern when doing so was to make sure that we could deliver products and services at a price and level of quality that would make us successful. For the first three years, we did nothing more than focus on building infrastructure, developing a flowing process to support the services for clients and creating a set of high-quality products. Looking back over that time, I would do things completely different. The first thing I would do if I was starting out today would be to develop a sales strategy for the company. My experience starting a company taught me that it is easier to build a product and the infrastructure to support it than it is to build an effective sales and marketing organization. Even in our tenth year of operation, we are still working diligently on building a more effective sales and marketing organization. In hindsight, the first hire I should have made was a head of sales and marketing. That would have accelerated the adoption of our products and services much faster than the approach we took. It is not just about having a good idea, or a great product; it is about how you convince clients to buy. This is done through creative marketing and sales. The way we sell our ideas inside the corporations we work for is no different. I now focus the majority of my time on working with the sales and marketing staff. The good news about my company is we built such a solid infrastructure that our product delivery and our costs are well within the range we defined from the start; the bad news is that it has become increasingly difficult in the marketplace to generate sales traction and we have had to devote all of our recent efforts to improving our sales and marketing.

Most entrepreneurs fall into the same trap I did. We typically have a background in technology rather than sales. This trend is even more pronounced in recent Internet companies that failed because they were led by technologists who ignored the need to develop a successful sales and marketing strategy. The most successful entrepreneurs are the ones who understand that their place is to build on an idea and find a partner to help them develop marketing and sales structures. They also recognize that every entrepreneur reaches a time when it is necessary to step back and bring in the next level of management talent to allow the company to grow. Very few entrepreneurs have been able to successfully turn an idea into a multi-billion-dollar corporation. We have all seen many examples of the failures, especially in the dot-com space; most failed because they were totally focused on their idea rather than on finding a market for that idea. Those who have been successful understood the need for their organizations to build a strong sales and marketing culture. As leaders, we must develop those cultures within our organizations. We need to create an environment of open communication, consistent messaging, and regular interaction with all areas of the organization. Without this sales effort, most of the good deeds of your team will go unnoticed.

We need to create an environment of open communication, consistent messaging, and regular interaction with all areas of the organization.

Sales Is Influencing Behavior

When you break sales down, it is really about influencing behavior. It is not pushing a product or trying to bang on doors and get people to buy the latest gadget, it is really about influencing the behavior of people to achieve an outcome you desire.

When you break sales down, it is really about influencing behavior.

When my son was beginning college he asked me for advice about what he should study. I told him to focus his efforts on sales and marketing. We talked a lot about how sales affects corporations and how no corporation can survive without sufficient sales. More importantly, we talked about leadership and where leaders come from. He went through an analysis of several major corporations tracing the background of their top executives and found that the majority of CEOs came from sales and legal areas and very few come from accounting and technical areas. This is because, as discussed throughout this book, leadership is about building relationships, working with people, and influencing behavior. All of which involve sales. The majority of CEOs come from sales because that background has allowed them to develop the tools and skills necessary to become influential leaders.

It is not that other areas of a corporation can't produce CEOs. Many, for example, come from the legal department. You need not look any further than Washington DC to see the number of lawyers who enter politics. Lawyers make for successful leaders for the same reason as people with a background in sales: They are taught early on to become good communicators and good persuaders. Many cases are won or lost through persuasion, performance, and influence. The best lawyers are often excellent orators.

The common skills all successful CEOs share are exceptional powers of communication and persuasion. I keep repeating that leadership is all about exceptional communication and the ability to influence the behavior of others. I have spent many meetings observing the behavior of the CEO and other leaders within the company and I have used those observations to help develop my own approach to leadership.

What Is Your Sales Style?

Developing a sales style is an individual thing. There is no set format or template. It is about how you can comfortably interact with others and influence them within your personal comfort zone. It isn't about being the most aggressive or loudest person in the room. It is about developing a style with which you are comfortable that allows you to engage and interact with others.

My wife and I have been married for over 45 years. The main reason our marriage has lasted is because our personalities are totally opposite. I am aggressive and driven while my wife is more passive and is happy to sit in the background. We recently moved from Connecticut to New Hampshire. As in all our moves, we joined a community where we didn't know anyone and had to start all over again building a network of friends and relations. This time was different though. I was not working for a corporation; I was working for myself and working out of my home office. We didn't have a corporate structure to help us create a core group of friends we could build on within the community. Instead, we looked for community organizations in which we both had an interest. My wife found the garden club and that changed everything for us.

After two years she was elected president of the club. During her two-year tenure, membership doubled, the finances of the club improved dramatically, and the exposure of the club in the community was massive. She was able to garner support from community leaders, some state leaders, and of course many of the members in the community through her efforts as president of the club. She achieved all of this in her subtle, quiet, and direct way. She has a knack for creating unique experiences at every monthly meeting. She brings props, games, and other tools to engage the audience. She never likes being in front of the group and she tries to create an environment where others share the spotlight. What she was able to do was create an environment where she was clearly viewed as a leader and everyone in the organization depended on her to help guide the organization. She did this through being herself rather than trying to change herself into the type of forceful leader you see in many organizations. Rather than mandate actions, she influenced people by building relationships with all the members of the club. She has an honest approach to everything she does that makes people feel comfortable working with her. She also was the first one to grab a shovel or dig up a plant or get her hands dirty to show others how work was done. This subtle type of leadership style is exactly what that club needed to succeed.

Today we have many friends and relationships in the community. We are members of dinner clubs, we are invited to several events around town each week, and my wife is now the official keeper of the town Christmas tree. All this was a direct result of her ability to make new friends by joining the garden club, becoming its leader, and making her mark in the community by leading from her comfort zone.

I mention this because, just like her, most of us in corporate life tend to be introverted and want to take the backseat rather than be the ones in the spotlight. We are not always comfortable being the one everyone looks to for advice or direction. The best way to move to that comfort zone is to examine what approaches to leadership fit naturally within your comfort zone and develop them into a leadership style that will allow you to lead in a way that feels natural.

My personal style is one of personal interaction. I always prefer to meet face to face rather than via phone or e-mail. I like to read people's reactions during a conversation as they tell you a lot about how the person is receiving your message and whether he or she can support it. Body language also tells you how comfortable someone is with the conversation in general. I find that dealing in this way, you can get much more accomplished. You also build stronger relationships.

When I was at my last corporate position, I was based in Connecticut and corporate headquarters moved to Chicago. I would visit there quite regularly. During these visits, I made it a point to never have lunch or dinner alone. I would always try to connect with one of my peers. You can gain quite a bit of information in a relaxed setting that you would never have been able to find out in a meeting. I always try to learn as much personal information about my peers as I can. These events were an invaluable tool in helping me build relationships and become a trusted business partner. Never underestimate the value of one-on-one interactions. Use them to your advantage to promote yourself and your business agenda. Make a personal commitment to reach out to others on a regular basis.

> Never underestimate the value of one-on-one interactions.

Everyone has a personal sales style. Your sales style is governed by your personality, background, experiences, and motivations. In some cases, it is also based on the observations of others. Just like our personalities, every one of us is unique in the way we approach promoting ourselves or our businesses.

Sales Is the Most Difficult Part of Starting a Business

When I started my own business, I thought I knew how to operate a business from being CEO of *Computerworld*, but I never fully understood the impact of being an entrepreneur. No one was there to help me, guide me, or show me the way. I had to fend for myself. In doing so, I made lots of mistakes. Looking back over the past 10 years in building my business, the consistent struggle was to find capable salespeople. I've become very cynical of salespeople based on my experiences over the past few years as an entrepreneur. Having been through many salespeople, commission strategies, and sales compensation plans, it became clear to me that salespeople are motivated differently than other leaders in the corporation. It is purely an emotional game with them. You need to keep them excited and engaged all the time. This is not the type of environment I experienced earlier in my career. I've learned more than I want to know about managing and operating a sales organization, but it's made me a far better leader having had that experience.

As mentioned earlier, every salesperson has a different style. The secret to success, though, is to help align this style with the culture you want to create at your company. Like anyone, when salespeople join the organization, they want to return to the comfort zone they developed at their previous job. This is a common occurrence in corporate life. When we start a new position, we always try to fall back a little bit to where we came from because that was our last point of comfort. This is true with salespeople as well. You need to help them break that mold so they can learn from the experiences they had and learn to apply those experiences to their current job. Rather than replicating where they came from, help them use that experience as a foundation to improve on at your company. This is exactly what we need to do ourselves as leaders.

If I had it to do over again, I would have spent much of the early part of my career understanding sales and how to sell. I never fully understood how being able to sell myself and my ideas could affect my career. When I compare myself to others, one of the largest impediments to advancement for any of us is an inability to sell ideas and influence others and their opinions. I talked a lot about relationships in the prior chapters, and I believe the ability to sell and influence is as important as the ability to build strong relationships. Had I understood this earlier in my career, I would have been much further ahead and been able to advance more rapidly because I would have developed my sales style earlier and not been forced to devote time later in my career to developing it.

Are You Trustworthy?

Trust is the foundation for all business relationships. Most of us take trust for granted and never take the time to understand the influence trust has on our daily lives. We've talked a lot about sales and developing a sales style, but in order to effectively promote and sell yourself you need to be trusted. Trust isn't instantaneous; it is built over time through both deeds and results.

Trust is the foundation to effective sales as well as personal relationships. It is the foundation of all of our interpersonal interactions. Do not underestimate the need to build trust before you try to sell yourself. One of my companies is a services firm. We spent many years trying to adjust our packaging and messaging to sell services more effectively only to realize that what we are selling is trust. We ask new customers to make substantial investments in a company run by people they don't know. We conducted several focus groups and everyone loved our business model, but they didn't know us and were reluctant to make a commitment to our services. They suggested that we move forward slowly, give them a chance to sample our services, and provide an opportunity to start small and then add services based on performance. This proved to be a turning point for our company.

> Trust is the foundation to effective sales as well as personal relationships. It is the foundation of all of our interpersonal interactions. Do not underestimate the need to build trust before you try to sell yourself.

We need to think about a similar model for building trust ourselves. Before you try the hard sell or to build a strong relationship, create small interactions with positive results. One way I have done this successfully is by demonstrating my understanding of the interests of the person with whom I want to connect. I will stop by and offer suggestions to someone about ways we might be able to work together to solve a specific problem. I will first convince the person that I have an intimate understanding of the problem at hand and then offer some constructive ideas to help. What I am doing is building trust by creating value. All you need is a couple of successes and you then have a strong foundation on which to build a trusting relationship. Like I have said before, you need to move in small steps. Everyone has a different pace in developing trust and you should try to move at the pace of the person you hope will trust you rather than at your own. Selling to someone is much easier after you have established a trusting relationship.

175

If you try to move to a selling posture before establishing trust, you are more likely to be rejected. To this day, I always make it a point to bring something of value to every meeting. You will find that once you develop a reputation for this, people will be much more willing to meet with you because you will have built a foundation of trust from which you can now sell to them.

Trust is the culmination of a series of interactions. I've talked a lot about relationships, networking, being a good presenter, and being a good salesperson throughout this book. In order to build a trusting relationship, you need to be effective at all of these. Trust is something that is easily lost and difficult to create. We've spoken about relationships and friendships and how important it is to be the one who reaches out to others. Trust is about that as well; about finding ways to demonstrate to others that you are trustworthy.

One of the easiest ways to do this is to admit your mistakes. People find it easier to trust those of us who aren't afraid to be upfront and honest when we make a mistake. When you make a mistake, you can build trust by admitting your faults to others and asking them to help you overcome them. We all know we are not perfect and that we have faults, so this is a safe way to begin building trusting relationships with others. Everyone has an inner desire to help others who reach out to them. This is the next logical step in creating a trusting relationship. We've taken the time to familiarize ourselves with each other, to work together, and to create value together; now it is time to take it to a more personal level. Trust is a personal thing and should not be taken lightly. You will find that exposing your vulnerabilities leads others to reciprocate and over time you not only work better together as a team, but you will each improve yourselves and overcome some of your weaknesses. Don't try to make a veiled attempt at this. Be sincere in your efforts and in your conversations. People can see right through deception and insecurity and you will never be able to build a trusting relationship around them.

> People find it easier to trust those of us who aren't afraid to be upfront and honest when we make a mistake.

Always tell the truth even when it hurts. Whenever I communicate with my staff or my peers, I make sure I can substantiate what I say and that it is the truth to the best of my knowledge. If I am unsure about something, I will not say it. There will be things you cannot discuss with your staff because of corporate regulations or security. During those times, I always tell people I'm not able to talk about the topic because it is too sensitive. For everything else, I always communicate as openly and directly as possible. As stated earlier, if I am unsure about an answer, I say so plainly and let the person know I will find the answer and provide it later. Don't answer for the sake of answering. It is okay to let people know that you don't know the answer but you will find it out and get back to them. Developing this kind of style will help you immensely in building trust with others.

Another way to build trusting relationships with others is to be consistent. When you are having a bad day, it is okay to admit it. You need to have honest and consistent communication to build consistent trust. You can't build trust when you don't have consistent behavior. People do not like uncertainty and insecurity, so it is important when building trust to let others know they can rely on you to respond clearly and consistently over time.

> Never compromise your values when building relationships. Always be yourself, always be consistent, and always be willing to help and share your experiences.

177

Think about the people in your career you did and did not trust. Consider what it was about each of them that shaped your opinion. We all have different personalities, backgrounds, and experiences. That is what makes life interesting and what makes building new relationships so much fun. The common thing we need to think about as we start to build trusting relationships both in the workplace and outside is that people are looking for us to be ourselves and not to try to mask ourselves to accommodate the situation. Trust is about honesty, consistency, and believability. Never compromise your values when building relationships. Always be yourself, always be consistent, and always be willing to help and share your experiences.

CHAPTER 10

Are You Ready to Make the Change?

C hanging jobs has become a way of life. Unlike previous generations of employees who worked for the same company for their entire careers, today the time we spend with companies is becoming increasingly shorter. Someone taking a leadership role in a corporation today spends an average of three to five years in that role. This is a dramatic change. The relationship we have with our employers today is strictly based on the value the job provides to our careers. I'm not saying I fully agree with this phenomenon; however, it is the way the world is. When people ask what my career is, I tell them I'm a corporate services provider. I enter a relationship with a corporation that lasts as long as I provide the services they require and they fairly compensate me for my work.

Professional sports epitomize this new culture. When I was a child, a baseball or basketball player often spent his entire career with one team. Just as in the corporate world, there is no longer a mutual sense of loyalty between the athlete and the team. It is the same in business—as long as the athlete continues to excel, he or she is retained by the team. As soon as that performance degrades in any way, the team looks to trade that person. Athletes are motivated by financial compensation; should another team present a better offer, the athlete could

179

join in a heartbeat. This is a part of our society today whether we like it or not.

Chapter 7 discussed how the Internet has affected our society in two major ways. First, it has created a culture of instant gratification: We no longer wait for things, we no longer have patience, and we want everything now. Second, it has created the phenomenon of personalization. Each one of us now expects to be treated as an individual in every aspect of our lives. These two phenomena also influence the relationship between employees and employers today.

> We have created a society where everything is temporary and we are always looking for the next best opportunity. This has led to an increase in mobility.

Loyalty, dedication, and devotion seem to have eroded over the years. This is very troubling because it affects our personal lives and those of our family members. We have created a society where everything is temporary and we are always looking for the next best opportunity. This has led to an increase in mobility; as we change employers we constantly move ourselves and our families. I have changed jobs several times in my career, as have most of my peers. When I changed jobs, it wasn't just me picking up and moving somewhere new, my family followed me to a new location, a different culture, and often a different climate. These changes can be both positive and negative. It is how you communicate them to yourself and your family that make them successful.

Both of my children have told me on several occasions they do not want to relocate the way our family did when they were growing up. They would like to remain in one place and one home as long as possible. This initially troubled me when I thought about it, but having spent several years mulling it over,

I believe frequent moves can have both positive and negative influences on your family and career. For example, my adult children have a different perspective on the world than they might have if I had stayed in one location for my entire career.

I grew up in New Hampshire, a small state with a rural culture. My first move was from New Hampshire to Florida. Aside from the big changes in culture and climate, we also moved from a rural area to an urban area. This was a profound change both for me and for my family. When I arrived in Florida, my initial reaction was one of worry about what I had done to myself and my family. Over the next few months as we bought a home, moved to a community, and became settled we grew more comfortable. My children were exposed to new cultures they had never encountered in New Hampshire. My daughter's best friend was a Cuban girl whose entire family had migrated from Cuba to south Florida. I remember my daughter visiting her friend's family functions and coming back to educate us about Cuban culture and foods. She would never have had this experience if we stayed in one place.

> Life is all about experiences. If you don't take the chance to make the move and experience different cultures and professional challenges, you may never fully understand the breadth of opportunities available to you.

My son was able to have similar experiences because of our moves. Aside from experiencing different cultures and climates, he was exposed to corporate culture. While he was in high school, he attended many corporate events with me. He was playing golf with CIOs and CEOs as a teenager. He attended events such as the Super Bowl and the Indianapolis 500 with me and my peers. These types of experiences prepared him to be the successful man he has become. Had we not taken the risk to make these moves, he may not have had a model for his success as an adult. Life is all about experiences. If you don't take the chance to make the move and experience different cultures and professional challenges, you may never fully understand the breadth of opportunities available to you.

I am not saying that remaining with the same company for your entire career is unacceptable in today's society, but that we have an increased opportunity to broaden our perspective through experiences when compared with employees a generation ago. Some people are very happy and remain with the same corporation. This is all part of your individual character and personality. Think about that when you are considering making any changes as you may not be as successful as you would like because a move disrupts your security or support mechanisms.

Getting Acclimated to the New Company

Every time I changed positions and went to a new company, I went through the same process. You start off in a position of total insecurity because you know little about your new company. I would sit in meetings and listen to my coworkers talk about new people, locations, and terminologies, trying to understand what they were talking about and how I could contribute to the conversation. These experiences taught me that the best approach to the first few weeks on a new job is to do a lot more listening than talking. Spend time understanding the nuances of the corporation you have just joined. What are the unique terms they use in expressing themselves? What is the organization's underlying culture? Who are the power brokers?

The process of acclimation is always the same. It would take me three to four months to begin feeling comfortable on the job. Even now, I remember the anxiety and fear associated with going to work each day at a new job. Was I ever going to understand the new company? Was I ever going to be accepted by my peers? In each case, there came a day when I suddenly could walk into the office and feel at ease with myself, the company, and my performance. When that happens, you know you have finally completed your transition. The timeframe can vary from company to company, but don't expect it to happen overnight.

> The first thing I always did when I accepted a new position was to find something that was broken that I could easily fix: a short-term success.

I learned more from each of my career changes than I had from the previous change. The first thing I always did when I accepted a new position was to find something that was broken that I could easily fix: a short-term success. In one position, the first thing I did was fix the e-mail infrastructure. The company had several e-mail systems that were talking to each other but making it difficult for humans to communicate. I found a software package that acted as a traffic cop—accepting messages from different packages and converting them to a standard format. This allowed me to simplify the e-mail system and provide a way for everyone to communicate easily. The political capital from this change lasted for over a year. It is important to find a short-term success wherever you go and use that to start gaining the respect of your peers and building relationships with other leaders.

One other thing I learned through my career was the importance of understanding where the power brokers were in the corporation. Every company has its power brokers; they could be the CEO, the CFO, or, as I found in many cases, the administrative assistants. I would spend time understanding the culture and where the power brokers were and begin to build relationships with them. This approach positions you for success at your new corporation. When I visited the manufacturing facilities, I would always take the time to talk to the plant manager, but I would spend more time on the factory floor with the people actually operating the machines. This approach allowed me to understand the operation of the manufacturing facility and gain the respect of those on the factory floor. Many times we had minor interruptions in our systems that could have been dramatic had I not had a relationship with the people on the factory floor. Instead of allowing systems to break down, they partnered with us and found ways to repair them so they operated more smoothly. As I discuss later in this chapter, you can only achieve this type of success by taking the time to build relationships with the power brokers at your company.

> One other thing I learned through my career was the importance of understanding where the power brokers were in the corporation.

Preparing for the Interview

I've always aggressively pursued new opportunities with a high level of intensity. Just like competing in a race where you are up against many others with the same objective, the thing that gives you an edge is preparation. Making sure the car is perfect, making sure every piece of equipment is operating flawlessly, and more importantly making sure you are mentally prepared for the competition ahead. This is the same way I used to prepare when I was interviewing for my next position. I looked at it as a competition: me against the rest of the candidates. It was important that I was able to differentiate myself as well as influence the person who was interviewing me by making a personal connection.

Interviewing for a new position is very time-consuming. You can't just walk in the door and take the interview; you need to spend a substantial amount of time preparing. Chapter 9 discussed selling yourself, and that is exactly what an interview is. You are preparing for a sales call where you are both the product and the one responsible for making the sale.

> Interviewing isn't just about seeking a job or looking for that next opportunity, it is about interacting with others in a way that allows you to influence their behavior. Interviewing is nothing more than a conversation.

Many people take the interview process too lightly. An interview is a good opportunity for you to both sell yourself, but also to learn from others. Interviewing isn't just about seeking a job or looking for that next opportunity, it is about interacting with others in a way that allows you to influence their behavior. Interviewing is nothing more than a conversation. People tend to get hung up about interviewing and feel emotionally strained just thinking about the interview process. Thinking about an interview as just another conversation helps relieve some of this strain. There are a few unique things to consider when preparing for an interview; otherwise, it really is just another conversation. One of the unique things about an interview is that your appearance—wearing the proper clothes and being well groomed—is much more important than in a regular conversation. One other unique element of the interview conversation is that you probably don't have a relationship with the other person like you would in a regular conversation, so it is important to engage your interviewer as much as you can. Doing so helps you learn about the interviewer so you can structure your responses in a manner that fits the interviewer's expectations.

Always remember that each of us is a unique individual with unique motivations. The way to influence behavior is to understand that uniqueness and use it to your advantage when communicating with others. An interview usually starts with some personal conversation; this is an important opportunity to learn about the people interviewing you. Use this time to ask them about themselves: how long they have been with the company, what they like about it, what they like to do outside of work. Gaining as much insight as you can up front allows you to position yourself and your responses in a way that will be persuasive to the interviewers. Don't discount how much one individual can influence this type of situation. The more you learn about your interviewers, the more you have an advantage over them in the dialogue. Think of interviews as interviews as opportunities to build new relationships with people you have never met before. The more you think about it that way and structure your responses accordingly the easier it will be for you to convey your points and for the interviewers to feel comfortable with your answers. It is not as difficult as you think to build a relationship while interviewing. Another great trick I always use is to watch the body actions of the people interviewing me. You can tell by the way they react to what you are saying whether they are interested, uninterested, or offended by what you say. Being observant can help you control the conversation.

> The more you learn about your interviewers, the more you have an advantage over them in the dialogue. Think of interviews as opportunities to build new relationships with people you have never met before.

Getting Comfortable in Your New Role

Every time I drive a new track for the first time I am uneasy about not knowing the terrain or the difficulty of the track. It is one thing to look at pictures in a magazines or online or to drive it on a computer simulation, but being there in person—strapping into the car and getting ready to go fast—is a whole different experience. I've learned the best way to break into a new track is to align yourself with others who have had success there. One thing about racing is the camaraderie the drivers share. Each driver is out to help other drivers get better because doing so helps everyone improve. Competition is about improving your game, but it also involves improving the game of your competitors as a way to continue to challenge yourself to improve. That is why most of the experienced competitors at a new track are more than willing to help you learn the track. I should add one caveat though: If you have a reputation for being a hothead or reckless, people will not help you. As stated in earlier chapters, the relationships and reputation you build over years determine how people react to you.

The first thing to do on your test day is to drive the track with a more experienced driver who can take you through what we call "slow on the racing line" laps. What that means is that you follow the same lines you would when racing at full speed, but you do so very slowly, adding speed as you gain knowledge of the track. Racing is all about knowing the nuances of the track, its breaking points, its turning points, and the apex of each corner. You will never develop that knowledge if you go out and go fast your very first time on the course. Young drivers will play the simulator games of the track many times before they actually see it, but as soon as they actually get to the track, they jump in the car and immediately try to drive the course as fast as possible. This wastes the whole weekend as they never really take the time to feel the track and gain an intimate understanding of its nuances. You can only learn a track by going out and driving it slowly, particularly if you can do this with an experienced driver who already knows the course. There is no substitute for experience, and getting yourself up to speed is a much more pleasant task if you are working with someone who has been there before.

Seeking out that experienced person, the one with an intimate knowledge of the facility, and the one who is willing to share that knowledge with you, is the most important thing you can do when you're experiencing a track for the first time. This also holds true in corporate life. You can't break into a new corporation by yourself. You also can't do it at full speed. You need to start slowly and take the time to understand the culture, the people, the motivations of your peers, and the identities of the power brokers. I will talk more about that later in this chapter. The important thing to remember as you break into a new position, as when you break onto a new track, is to find someone who has been there before. This can take time. Don't try to solve all the problems or make a huge impact the first day. The faster you start, the longer your learning process will be. Slowing down and taking the time to integrate yourself into a new company gives you the knowledge you need to succeed in the long run.

> Slowing down and taking the time to integrate yourself into a new company gives you the knowledge you need to succeed in the long run.

Finding an experienced guide to help you integrate into a new company is a tall task. Just as I stated before, you need to slowly integrate yourself into the company. Finding the right person or persons to assist you with this process will take time. When you first start a new position the best approach is to spend your first few days or even weeks meeting with your peers, learning their priorities, learning about them as individuals, and developing an understanding of their history with the company and their knowledge of the company. I've learned to really take my time as I introduce myself and start to build relationships with others. In a lot of cases in corporate life people tend to exaggerate their successes, their knowledge of the company, and their level of influence within the corporation. You need to spend time sorting through each one of these introductions to ensure you align yourself with the right people. Knowing how to identify these people is not something you can gain from a textbook—it is something you need to understand from experience. I have been burned several times in my career by making the wrong initial choices. The way I overcame this was by taking more time to really understand each individual I met and comparing new people to people I already knew. I began formulating in my own mind the right set of traits or ideas I was looking for. It's human nature for all of us to try to exaggerate our importance. We need to recognize that and admit it is a common trait among most people in corporate life today. Understanding that makes it easier for you to synthesize the feedback you receive from others and form a realistic opinion of people and their value to you as you integrate into a new company.

> When you first start a new position the best approach is to spend your first few days or even weeks meeting with your peers, learning their priorities, learning about them as individuals, and developing an understanding of their history with the company and their knowledge of the company.

After you have selected the individuals you feel can best assist you with your integration, the next thing to do is develop an understanding of the major challenges facing the organization. Working primarily in IT, there has never been a shortage of problems or complaints about services, so I always found a target-rich environment when I started a new position. Having said that, the best opportunity for you when you change jobs is to go into a company where things really aren't working well at all. That gives you the opportunity to demonstrate dramatic and rapid results and influence the organization in a positive way. After having a detailed discussion with my peers, I typically create a priority list of items that need to be addressed. The first thing I do is find that one problem that is both fairly easy to fix and highly visible because it will generate a big return to the corporation. When you walk in the door as a new member of the management team being able to immediately generate tangible results helps you build relationships and respect more quickly than taking the safe road and analyzing issues for months before acting on them. This involves some risk but it can be greatly mitigated by taking the time to build the right relationships with the right people and gaining the right understanding of the real issues the corporation faces.

The next step in integrating yourself into a company is what I would call the "PMCC rule"—PMCC standing for *products, markets, customers, and competitors*. Executives today never take the time to gain enough knowledge about the company for which they work. I know this sounds absurd, but if you interviewed a lot of top executives you would find this to be true in a lot of cases. Most of us tend to focus on our own areas and ignore those managed by others. In order to be an effective corporate leader, you need to gain an intimate understanding of all operations of the business.

In order to be accepted as a member of the new team, it is imperative that you talk in their language, understand their concerns, and work cooperatively with them on solutions. This requires an intimate knowledge of your company's operations and products. Your staff also needs to have this intimate knowledge. When I manage a large organization, I enforce the PMCC rule with every employee. I personally question people about our largest competitor, our most profitable product, our least profitable product, where we are vulnerable to the competition, and other important aspects of the company. In order to be successful and effective in their day-to-day jobs, every member of the corporation must share this knowledge. The best organizations are those where everyone is operating from the same knowledge and can contribute in a meaningful and productive manner.

> The best organizations are those where everyone is operating from the same knowledge and can contribute in a meaningful and productive manner.

While I was working for a major retail products manufacturer, we had a distribution center that prepared two types of loads for tractor-trailers. One was what we called a full load and the other was a list of load or LTL. The full part of the business was operating very efficiently; we could load trucks in under an hour and get them on their way. The LTL side was not. It took several hours to load LTL trucks, which left us with trucks lined up to the highway waiting to take on loads. When this happened, many drivers would abandon us and go somewhere else rather than wait the multiple hours it would take to load their vehicles. Having knowledge of the warehousing systems and the distribution process of our company, we were able to propose a very simple solution. What we did was locate an unused area within the distribution center and mark off a tractor-trailer sized space in masking tape. We could then use this space to stage the loads for the LTLs. We already knew that our warehouse distribution system would allow us to stage loads in multiple locations, which made it easy for us to track material automatically. By doing this, we could reduce the LTL load time from four or five hours to less than an hour. This one simple solution solved the backlog problem at the distribution center and allowed us to have a much freer flow of products. These are the types of solutions you can provide your company when you gain an intimate understanding of its operations.

Understanding the Culture

After you make a commitment to a new company and prepare yourself for the integration process, you're ready to begin your journey. It starts with gaining an understanding of the organization's culture, its language, and the power brokers within the organization. This understanding helps you develop a comprehensive model that allows you to be competitive.

The first thing to do is relax. You're not going to learn everything in one day or one week. It will take time for you to feel comfortable within the company. I once went to work for a family-owned organization reporting to the son of a founder. From day one, it became apparent that most people stayed with this company for their entire careers. Its long-tenured personnel had developed a family culture throughout the organization, which made my acclimation process more difficult. It took a significant amount of time for me to gain acceptance. This is an initial hurdle that too many leaders underestimate: They want to become fully engaged in the day-to-day operations before taking the time to understand the underlying culture of the company.

All companies have a specific structure, a specific point of evolution, and a historical background that define where they are today. All these ingredients go into the company's culture, and any new leader must gain an intimate understanding of each of them. You cannot effectively implement the improvements and efficiencies you were recruited to complete without first tying them to the company's culture and presenting them in a way that lets people understand that link.

While every company has an overriding culture that sets the theme for the entire organization, you will also find several subcultures within each organization, and you'll need to gain an understanding of these as well. A leader gets things done through teamwork and by working within the cultural boundaries of the organization. You'll find it best to engage personnel in the culture where they feel comfortable and where they have succeeded in the past. You may not always approve of the culture, but you should initially embrace it. You cannot expect to walk into a corporation and immediately change its culture. You can't recreate your previous environment, but you can apply lessons from your past experiences to your new company. Over time, as you gain respect and achieve successes, you may want to accept the challenge of trying to mold a new corporate culture, but this cannot be undertaken initially—it must be planned and achieved over the long term.

> You can't recreate your previous environment, but you can apply lessons from your past experiences to your new company.

Learning the Language

Part and parcel of each company's culture is its unique language. Every industry has its own technical jargon, but within specific industries, each corporation has its own internal language as well. Certain terms and means of communication are unique to the company. This internal language evolves over time and combines colloquialisms, industry jargon, and specific terms unique th that specific company. It is imperative that any new leader gain an intimate fluency in this language and an understanding of its etymology—how it originated and evolved to where it is today.

In order to be accepted as part of a company, you need to speak its language and understand the intricacies of its culture. Much of the integration process involves overcoming your colleagues' perception of you as an outsider. The sooner you can transition yourself from outsider to team member, the sooner you can become productive and implement your goals.

> It is imperative that any new leader gain an intimate fluency in this language and an understanding of its etymology—how it originated and evolved to where it is today.

To begin, spend some time—a few days, weeks, or however long it takes—sitting down with the leadership team and listening to them. Ask questions about their history with the corporation, their concerns, and what they see as opportunities and challenges for the company. This accomplishes two objectives. First, it enhances your personal relationship with each member of the leadership team, which is a critical step in effectively integrating yourself into the culture. (Remember: This book is all about developing strong relationships in order to become successful.) Second, it helps you gain a more intimate understanding of the company's language, its history, and the internal challenges it has undergone. During these meetings, ask questions and do a lot of listening. The purpose of these interviews is for you to learn about the company and its people, not for you to talk about yourself. That can come later, after you have learned to express yourself in words that relate to the company rather than to you as a person, in terms that everyone in the corporation understands.

In order to be understood, you must communicate in a language and with a set of references that your listeners comprehend. To take an example from my racing career, when my crew chief radios to ask how the car is performing, I need to respond in a language he understands. I might say that I'm having a "high-speed entry push" or "exit oversteer" or "no mechanical grip" on a specific area of the track. My crew chief understands these terms, and we share a mutual understanding of the specific problem as we try to resolve it. Effective communication can make the difference between winning and losing, both in racing and in the corporate arena. In order to become more competitive, your team members need a mutual understanding of the objective and of any obstacles that must be overcome. If you cannot effectively communicate the issues confronting your team, you will never accomplish your goal.

> In order to be understood, you must communicate in a language and with a set of references that your listeners comprehend.

In addition to gaining an intimate understanding of the company's language, you must also ensure that everyone in your organization shares your fluency and that they communicate in that language during all of their internal and external interactions. I think of the many physicians with whom I've interacted through the years. The best experiences have occurred with doctors who could convey in understandable terms any medical diagnoses they were making. Those who spoke in strictly medical terms somehow made me feel that neither of us had a clear understanding of the issue at hand or how we might resolve it. This same phenomenon holds true in corporate life. We each have an intimate understanding of the intricacies and technologies involved in our organizations; and when we

195

interact with people outside our organization, we must communicate in a manner that fosters a mutual understanding of the problem we're trying to solve. This takes patience and fortitude. It may also take a little more time, but in the long run you will gain more by communicating effectively than by trying to rush ahead without a shared understanding among members of your team.

To ensure that everyone in your organization speaks the company's language, try to use that language in all your conversations with team members. I understand there are times when specific terminologies relevant to your area of the organization require you to communicate in those terms; however, keep these to a minimum. Your objective is to have your entire team thinking in the language of the corporation rather than thinking in their specific technical terms. Many years ago I lived in Germany and tried to learn German. I found myself translating everything I heard from German to English and English to German, and it soon became apparent the only way I was going to learn German was to think in German, not English. This is also the case in your professional life: You must think in the language of your corporation and not translate from one language to another.

> You must think in the language of your corporation and not translate from one language to another.

You will be surprised how quickly you'll gain the respect and support of your peers when they see that you are attempting to address them in their language. When I was in Germany, I never mastered the language, even though I tried desperately to learn it. I did learn, however, that German people were far more cooperative when I attempted to communicate in their language than when I tried to engage them in English. The fact that I made the attempt demonstrated a sincerity that allowed me to build relationships with them and to achieve the goals I had set out for myself. You don't need to become fluent in the company's language before communicating, but you need to let everyone know that you are taking the time to learn it. You'll find that people will be more than eager to work with you. We have all heard the phrase "perception is reality." I firmly believe that the language in which we communicate directly affects how we are perceived.

Identifying and Building Relationships with Power Brokers

While understanding the company's culture and language is extremely important, the way you get things done is by recognizing the organization's power brokers. These are people who have respect throughout the organization and the ability to influence its decisions. They can be administrative assistants, plant managers, key factory floor workers, or a host of other positions. Never assume that all the power resides at the top of the organizational chart. In almost every corporation, the true power brokers work several levels down from the top. It is extremely difficult to implement change or improvements in any organization without first gaining the support of the power brokers. If you cannot convince them of the merits of your initiative, you will not succeed.

> Never assume that all the power resides at the top of the organizational chart. In almost every corporation, the true power brokers work several levels down from the top.

I remember attempting to implement a new shop-floor control system at a manufacturing company. The head of manufacturing and the plant management were on board, and we were ready to roll out the new application at the individual plants. However, I knew that the people who operated the major machinery were the real power brokers at those plants. The machinery required voluminous technical manuals, repair guides, and service updates as part of operation and maintenance. These power brokers didn't need any manuals for the existing machines; they could assess a machine's efficiency and maintenance status by its sound alone. They knew the volume of material that had passed through the machines, when a machine needed maintenance, when it was about to break down, and when it needed upgrading. Without including these power brokers in the decision-making process, the implementation would not work: There was no way we could introduce a new control system without their support. Even though none of the power brokers worked for me, I spent the majority of my time working with them, listening to their ideas, gaining their support, and helping them assume ownership of the project. As a result, we effectively implemented the system at every manufacturing facility throughout the corporation with the complete support of the factory personnel.

I have seen many similar initiatives fail because the organization did not take the time to embrace and engage its power brokers. Every new initiative you try to implement within an organization has a chance of success or failure. The way to ensure success is by recognizing, involving, and gaining the support of the company's power brokers. Take the time to understand who and where these people are within your new organization. Meet with them and establish personal relationships. Then consult with them and keep them engaged in as many of your activities as you possibly can.

In order to effectively build relationships with power brokers, you need to have that PMCC—products, markets, customers, competitors—understanding of your corporation so you can carry on an intelligent conversation that provides value. Being able to speak their language gives them confidence that you understand the intricacies of the business and allows you to build a relationship based on trust. I have watched several successful CEOs throughout my career, and each one has had an intimate understanding of who the real power brokers were in the company and has built strong personal relationships with each of them. The unsuccessful leaders are those who never took the time to understand these power structures. They would work with leaders at certain levels but ignore the company's culture and the true source of its decisions.

A good rule of thumb is to start with the administrative assistants, especially the ones who have been there the longest. I have found through my experience that they wield a lot more power than you might think. In addition, they tend to have a clear understanding of the company's culture and the people who wield the most power. The next place I always go is to the long-term employees. In one of my positions, there were people who were third-generation employees. I would always try to seek these people out as they are the ones who can give you the best history of the company, as well as the best perspective on the real challenges it faces today.

Integration Is an Ongoing Process

You have taken the time to learn the products, markets, customers, and competitors. You have identified the major challenges and quick fixes to address several of them. You have developed a strong understanding of the company's culture and language and identified and reached out to its power brokers. At this point, your integration is well under way. The culture of a company determines how things are accomplished;

understanding that culture greatly improves the likelihood that your future initiatives will succeed.

> Just like building relationships, though, integrating yourself into a company's culture is an ongoing process.

Just like building relationships, though, integrating yourself into a company's culture is an ongoing process. Culture is a living thing in corporations just as in our society. Staying abreast of changes, building relationships with the power brokers driving those changes, and remaining open to new ideas and approaches to your work are essential for continued success. The more you immerse yourself in the culture and language surrounding you and the more you build relationships with others throughout the corporation, the better you will be able to achieve your goals and those of the corporation for years to come.

CHAPTER 11

Today's New World and How We Cope

One point I have not discussed at length is the pace of change and how it affects us and our society. Understanding this phenomenon is critical to leaders making business decisions—and also critical to all of us as we make decisions in our personal lives as well. The Internet has had a tremendous effect on society and, more specifically, on the way we lead. The two major expectations it has created—instant gratification and personalization—have created an impatient society, one that demands personal attention. We need to understand how these expectations affect our lives and businesses.

> The Internet has had a tremendous effect on society in general and, more specifically, on the way we lead. The two major expectations it has created—instant gratification and personalization—have created an impatient society, one that demands personal attention.

During my 40-plus years of corporate life, I've seen profound changes in both the corporate and the social environments. Years ago business was simpler. We were less distracted by outside stimuli than we are today, and we operated with less information and at a more leisurely pace. We could take more time making decisions, face fewer options, and consider those options in greater depth. Today rapid change is a part of our daily lives. With each passing year, the pace of change increases. Moreover, we are confronting information overload. We have created an environment in which we are constantly flooded with information—some valuable, some worthless—and we're increasingly required to make critical decisions instantly.

Even world economic cycles are getting shorter, and this directly influences our planning and decision-making processes. Long-term strategic planning is now measured in months rather than years. Wall Street has been driving this for years. It forces us to make decisions based on quarterly performance rather than decisions based on success over time. The common perception in this environment is that short-term profits are more important than long-term strategy. As leaders, we need to resist this perception and find a way to balance the demand for instantaneous decisions with the necessity for careful strategic planning over the longer term.

The Influence of the Internet

The Internet has profoundly affected the way we live and the way we perform our jobs. It has created two phenomena in our daily lives. The first is instant gratification. Online we grow impatient with computer-response times of more than five or six seconds. This impatience spills over into the corporate world as well. The other phenomenon is personalization. Companies such as Amazon have created environments in which we feel we are recognized as individuals. In the corporate world, people want that same personal accommodation—and they want it now!

Instant Gratification

Instant gratification and personalization are now the controlling factors in society. We are an impatient society. Signs of this impatience are all around us: the car horns blown seconds after a light turns green, the billboards outside many local hospitals displaying the expected wait to see a doctor, the driver next to you checking her e-mail on a mobile phone while sitting at a stop light. I've already written at length about the need to slow down and be more observant, but the message you receive in most cases is exactly the opposite. The barrage of information in our daily lives and the expectation of instant gratification are major problems for leaders today. Leadership is not a quick and easy skill to master; it is based on years of gaining experience, building trust, and nurturing relationships. There is no shortcut to successful leadership. Success requires you to fight the urge to solve every problem today and focus on positioning yourself and your company to make the right decisions for the future.

> There is no shortcut to successful leadership. Success requires you to fight the urge to solve every problem today and focus on positioning yourself and your company to make the right decisions for the future.

We need to become more patient and remember the importance of personal interactions. We are constantly checking our e-mails and voicemails; we can't go anywhere without our cell phones. In many cases, we are ignoring those closest to us for the sake of checking e-mail. I have watched couples in a restaurant sit there and check their e-mails while waiting for dinner instead of having a conversation with each other. This is not the way you build relationships. It is sad that we have allowed our lives to be ruled by our electronic devices. I know I sound old-fashioned, but I still believe that business gets done by people working with people rather than by people working with devices. The young generation uses cell phones as their primary communication mechanism. Despite all this electronic interaction, the younger generation is starting to understand the need for more personal interaction. Remember the television commercial described in Chapter 8? Those young people searching for a campsite by driving until they lose cellular service typifies this growing understanding. Don't let the ease and convenience of electronic communication make you forget what is most important. Embrace technology, but remember that leadership is about person to person interaction.

The need for instant gratification has consumed society. I don't have to look any further than my wife. She is one of the most patient people I know; however, put her in front of a computer and she totally changes. When the computer does not respond within her threshold, which is probably about five seconds, she starts pushing other keys. Her lack of patience disrupts the operation of her computer—leaving her dead-ended in programs I never knew existed and functions I have never seen. Her desire to go faster actually slows her down, and I then get the call for help. The Internet has changed her behavior by giving her an expectation of instant gratification.

Personalization

The requirement for personalization has also affected the way we lead and conduct business. In college, we used to discuss market segmentation. We would divide the market into large sectors based on behavior and buying patterns. Everything we created was targeted to a specific sector. We studied demographics extensively and would use them in planning our product promotions. We would even use statistical sampling techniques to determine product performance and requirements. With the advent of the Internet, much of this work has been abandoned in favor of techniques that are less speculative. For the first time, we can actually measure the effectiveness of our advertisements by counting click-throughs and other metrics.

While I was CEO of *Computerworld* magazine, we were going through the transition from all-print to a combination of print and on-line advertising. After our advertisers saw the additional value provided by on-line advertisements, the migration from print rapidly accelerated. You only have to look at all the newspaper failures to see the effects of this change. It has also had a tremendous influence on revenue as well. A full-page advertisement in print was about $14,000 and the same advertisement on-line was about $1,500. The Internet had changed the marketing game.

The smart companies have taken it to a new level by introducing predictive analytics. What these do is observe past individual behavior and predict future buying interests. Amazon's site, with its personalized suggestion engine, is a prime example of this approach to selling goods. Each time you log on you are welcomed and guided through the site with suggestions based on your personal purchase history, your recent browsing on the site, and your additions to a personal wish list. Every purchase is followed by recommendations for additional purchases related either to the item you just bought or to other items similar to the one you just bought based on the purchase histories of users Amazon deems similar to you. The site attempts to give you the impression of a personal concierge. Hotels and airlines are following suit. We have now reached the point where most sites cater to the needs of their individual visitors, and this will continue to be a growing trend that shapes future business.

We need to think about this as we lead. People are starting to demand the same experiences on Monday morning at work that they had all weekend on-line. These are forces too strong to change or ignore, so you need to embrace them in order to maintain the respect of your employees. The best way to address these expectations is through collaboration. Discuss them openly and ask for your team's help in finding ways to address them. Get your team engaged and together build a culture that supports collaboration. In doing this, you will gain their respect, and, even more important, build a stronger team. You need to set the stage for the rest of the enterprise. Get out in front of these developments and be a leader. I always tell the leaders I coach that the smart leaders are out in front of changes rather than waiting for others to take the lead. An example of this is how smart CIOs in previous decades researched outsourcing and had answers to questions about how it could help their companies before the questions were asked. This is how to become a trusted partner and demonstrate leadership within your company and across your industry. Creating the right environment and platform to enable individual behavior is imperative. This is probably one of the largest challenges facing corporations today, and the challenge only grows as time goes on. Better to get out in front of it before it overcomes you.

> I always tell the leaders I coach that the smart leaders are out in front of changes rather than waiting for others to take the lead.

What Is the Market Looking for in a Leader?

Leading in this new world requires that you become more of an influencer rather than one who mandates. Companies are looking for a new model for leadership; they are looking for "game changers," leaders with vision and big ideas. Today, more than ever before, survival is based on the organization's ability to react to new markets, modify direction, and be more creative. As I have discussed, the pace of change is so rapid that new leaders need to be able to embrace change and adjust their style to keep up. At the same time, leaders must balance change with strategies developed to ensure sustained future success.

> Companies are looking for a new model for leadership; they are looking for "game changers," leaders with vision and big ideas.

You need to instill this visionary culture in your team. You should strive to create an environment that rewards creativity while not punishing mistakes made in good faith. In order to be creative, we all make mistakes. Too many organizations fail to develop a culture that embraces risk taking rather than punishing it. Research organizations fail many times before they get it right, and even successful inventors have frequent failures in their portfolios. The younger generation expects to work in an environment that allows for mistakes, and punishing members of your team for mistakes that arise from creative efforts will end up stifling future creativity. As mentioned earlier, I tell my people that a person who doesn't make mistakes isn't trying; but it is not acceptable to keep making the same mistake. I have also tried to foster creativity by creating competitions between organizations for innovative ideas with small rewards to the winner. Pharmaceutical companies fail more than they succeed, but they have created an environment that understands and supports failed initiatives because they are part of a larger creative process. We all need to develop the right creative culture in our own organizations.

Companies today are looking for leaders who are client-focused and display a proven track record of creating better client solutions than the competition. I know this sounds strange, but you would be surprised how many companies pay more attention to their product development efforts than to their clients' needs. They also seem to spend more time focused on the competition than on the market. The fact that we live in a world of rapid change requires us to continually monitor changes in market and client behavior. The shelf life for products and ideas is shorter and shorter. As a leader, you need to make sure you have an infrastructure and organization that is sensitive to and can react to changes in the market. You also need to have a deep bench of ideas for introduction. All of these things are part of being a visionary. This is a great opportunity for you to work more closely with your peers to share ideas and initiate mutual projects. You can't find a better way to build relationships and trust.

You must be willing to be accountable for good and bad in order to gain trust. We don't get it right every time and we need to stand up and admit our mistakes. This also holds true for your team. Everyone wants to have a leader who will stand up for them in good and bad. Honesty and integrity start with accountability.

> You must be willing to be accountable for good and bad in order to gain trust... Honesty and integrity start with accountability.

The Distributed Workplace

The leadership model today is significantly different from what it was when I started my career. Spans of control are greater, organizations are becoming flatter, and structural barriers of the past are being taken down. Individual workers throughout companies are empowered today in a way workers have never been before. In addition, many organizations today have a disbursed geographical structure with employees spread across multiple corporate buildings, home office, and coffee shops either about town or across the globe. This distribution requires a different management style. Teams now work remotely and collaborate via video and teleconferences. Companies are looking for leaders with a demonstrated ability to produce productive organizations. This is not easy; it takes time to develop an organization, instill a shared culture, and establish personal relationships when your employees are remote. You begin by developing basic rules for engagement: meeting formats, team structure, roles and responsibilities, a comprehensive action plan, and a governance structure to manage demand and prioritization. Then you develop an extensive communications plan.

Cultural differences can cause some organizational tension. Most organizations today have three generations of workers. Each generation has differing expectations. These differences can cause tension. Left unaddressed, they may get out of control. In addition to dealing with multiple generations, we have to integrate workers from multiple cultures. Most organizations span the globe, adding more complexity to the cultural mix. We need to develop new leadership styles that can manage the challenges that come with these changes. The best way to address them is head on. When working with a remote team I had the team members begin a matrix of cultural traits we identified as we worked together. We then held team discussions about the traits we identified. The team members explained why they acted the way they did and educated the rest of the team about where this behavior came from. We talked about the origins of holidays, family structures, corporate organizational structures, and behavioral traits. The next step was to collaborate on how we could adapt our interactions to acknowledge these differences. In some cases, just talking openly about our cultural differences left open the opportunity for behavioral change and understanding on both sides. Left unaddressed, the team could not function, but faced in this way, we became more cohesive and better able to work together.

I was recently working with a major corporation that was moving to a new headquarters. When they designed the facility, they did not provide offices for the entire staff. They created transient workspaces and encouraged selected groups to work remotely. This can cause management challenges. One of the first things they did was to create a set of policies for working at home. For example, one of the policies was that anyone using child care before working at home was expected to continue using it while working at home. Another one was that you were expected to work eight hours per day. Everyone was required to sign a contract that outlined the work-at-home policies. The best way to lead these types of organizations is to have a comprehensive reporting process that includes performance milestones. In addition, you need to have regular meetings physically bringing together as many members of the team as possible. A good rule is probably to bring them all together at least once a quarter. Project teams should be brought together in subgroups based on milestones. Make sure that you personally touch base with them on a regular basis as well.

Create a Plan for You

I have spent the entire book talking about my experiences. Now it is time for you to take the reins. You need to think about what is next for you. How are you going to prepare yourself for the next opportunity? In this chapter, I would like to offer some suggestions. They are generic and provided to get you thinking about finding the best route for you. It is now time for you to get personal and try to bring the thoughts and recommendations you have been reading together in a model that will serve your personal needs. The important thing is that this is more than a one-time exercise. It needs to become an integral part of your daily activities from here on. In order to become an effective leader, it is imperative that you devote a certain amount of your time to honing your leadership skills. All too many times we start things out with good intentions and then abandon them. The difference between being a successful leader and failing is a lack of effort. When Michael Jordan was playing for the Chicago Bulls, his coach would always say that he was the first one to arrive at practice every day and the last one to leave. It was no secret why he excelled at what he did. He understood the dedication it took to be the best and was willing to do whatever it took to succeed. We need to learn these kinds of lessons ourselves in corporate life. There is no difference between excelling in sports and excelling in leadership and corporate life. It is all about the commitment and the dedication that we make as individuals.

Just like business, racing requires dedication, practice, and devotion. It is about developing your reflexes, your concentration, and your physical being. In order to excel, you need to have what we call seek time. What this means is time in the car on the track going through multiple testing and training sessions to help you understand the feel of your car, recognize its limitations, and constantly try new things to improve your speed and grip on the track. It is this constant effort to improve, find a faster way, and wring the most out of yourself and the car that makes you successful as a racecar driver. The next thing you need to do is always look for better drivers than yourself to compete with. You will never improve yourself unless you're competing with others who are more experienced and better than you are. It is this constant internal desire to improve that drives a successful racecar driver. These lessons are also true in the corporate world. You need to continually try to improve yourself and find those leaders you want to emulate. You need to observe their behaviors, understand what makes them successful, and use that as the foundation for making yourself a better leader. You will never know how good you can be unless you compete with the best.

> You will never know how good you can be unless you compete with the best.

Become a Mentor Yourself

In my current role, I act as a mentor and coach to several senior executives. I have found this experience extremely rewarding. It makes me feel good to know I can use my decades of experience to help others. It feels great to give back and help others be more successful than I was. Every one of these experiences makes me a better person as well. No two people and no two situations are the same, so mentoring is a learning experience for me as well as for the person I am mentoring. Through this type of experience you build strong bonds and strong relationships that can last for years. These are the kinds of bonds and relationships that drive my desire to consistently improve and do a better job. I always feel I'm not doing enough for the people I am mentoring, and I spend a large amount of my personal time finding ways I can create more value for them from our relationships. There is some pressure when you know you are the one expected to be giving guidance and demonstrating leadership; however, I have found that, as we develop strong personal relationships, it becomes more of a sharing experience than one of me as the sole teacher. The most rewarding times as a coach and a mentor are when you watch the professionals you have been working with move up and excel in their careers. I don't think there can be a more rewarding experience other than seeing your children excel. I strongly suggest that as you develop yourself as a leader and improve your leadership skills you reach out and start to mentor others.

A good place to start would be with sports or other community organizations to which your children might belong. It is a safe place for you to test your mentoring skills as well as an opportunity for you to build better relationships with your children. Even if you don't have children of your own, finding an opportunity to mentor children provides a safe environment for you to hone your skills and make mistakes. Children are much more forgiving than adults and you also have the opportunity to learn from the other volunteers in the organization. As my children were growing up, I always found the time to be involved in their activities. Even though I wasn't able to teach my daughter how to dance or know all of the intricacies of football for my son, I was always a member of the parent associations. Through that experience I was able to make a whole new set of friends, and more importantly learn how to become a leader. The added benefit was that it showed my children I cared about them enough to make time to be involved. As I said before, this is a double win.

These types of experiences can be trying: When you're dealing with parents in competitive situations, there is always tension. There is nothing worse than an upset football mom. I remember one time, while I was the president of my son's football league, a mother was upset about how much playing time her son received. She was rather belligerent and demanding. The first thing I did was make her aware of how her behavior was affecting the kids as well as the poor impression she was making on the other parents. I arranged for her to meet with the coach and me and we had a very honest and open meeting. We listened to her concerns and then explained our position. I then followed up with a personal meeting with her. We discussed her behavior and how it affected her son and the other kids. I also pointed out to her that this wasn't just about athletics, but also about teamwork. We were trying to help her son and the players build a strong foundation for their personal growth. She listened and agreed. I was able to diffuse her concerns and change her perspective about the objective of the league. She eventually became my biggest supporter. We developed a great friendship and, more importantly, her son grew into a great young adult.

Youth sports, incidentally, was a tremendous training ground for me and you should consider it as well. The great thing about getting involved in these kinds of organizations is they allow you to learn how to deal with tensions and human interactions in an environment outside the workplace where you are not worried about being threatened by superiors or negatively affecting your career. It is a wonderful opportunity for you to learn about the behavioral characteristics of others and be able to hone your management skills as you try to convince others to support your positions. This is all about the salesmanship, marketing, and leadership that I've talked about in previous chapters. It is an opportunity for you to bring all of these skills together and build on them in a very constructive and positive way for yourself and others.

Learn to Present to the Interest of the Audience

In Chapter 9, I spoke about being a member of the Jaycees organization. I used that opportunity as well as being involved with community and children's activities to hone my presentation and speaking skills. I strongly suggest that you take advantage of the opportunities provided by this type of organization. One of the largest areas for improvement in leaders today is in perfecting their speaking and presenting skills; every leader today must become an effective presenter and speaker. Being a leader and building trust with others can only be accomplished through effective communication. Safe environments like the Jaycees allow

you to develop your individual style and your individual character. These are experiences that you can immediately translate
into your daily corporate life.

I've not spent much time talking about effective presentations and communications. Nevertheless, you need to understand the most effective means of communicating with the different levels of management you must address. I learned this
lesson when I made my first PowerPoint presentation in a board
meeting. I was asked to give the status of the major multimillion-
dollar project that we were undertaking and it required constant
board review and approval. I put together a presentation of approximately 14 slides with a set of handouts for board members.
I went to my boss at the time and reviewed the presentation with
him and it was an eye-opening experience for me. The first thing
he told me was that when you are presenting at the board level
you should never have more than four slides. Have all the information in your pocket to back up the slides should questions
be raised, but never have more than four slides. The other thing
he told me was never to give out any paperwork to board members. Anything you hand out enters the record for the meeting.
They would much rather have all of their materials in one brief-
ing package rather than provided as separate handouts. In many
cases, boards operate from multiple locations so it is important
that all of the information they need be clear, concise, and in
one place. The lesson I learned from this was that the amount
of detail you present is directly proportionate to the level of the
people to whom you are presenting. The lower the level of
the audience, the more detail they are looking for. The higher
the level of the audience, the more summarization of information is required. When you reach the board level, what they
really want is exception reporting. They only want to understand the items about which they need to make decisions and
they are not concerned with anything running smoothly. Remember, as you develop your speaking and presentation skills,

to understand your audience and adjust the level of the content to match their expectations. When you demonstrate your ability to provide people the information they need on a regular basis, you will get a reputation as someone people look forward to engaging.

> When you are presenting at the board level, you should never have more than four slides. Have all the information in your pocket to back up the slides should questions be raised, but never have more than four slides.

It goes without saying that you also need to rehearse your speeches and presentations several times before making them. It makes you much smoother in front of the audience and much more sincere and believable. I remember one time during my career I was struggling to create a memo and I went to my boss and asked him for some advice. He said that I should write like I speak, in my own language and using my own style, because doing so makes it easier to write and get my point across. I can't tell you how great that coaching was for me. Since that time, I've always remembered that in everything I write, including my speeches and presentations. Whether I'm writing a memo, giving a speech, or making a presentation I always do it in a way that is consistent with my style and my delivery. The message here is that if you try to be yourself whenever you communicate with others or make a presentation, you'll be much better received. You will also find that you're much more comfortable in front of an audience when what you are saying is in your natural voice.

Another great experience I've had over the years is teaching. For the past 15 years I have volunteered as a speaker at several universities. Like mentoring and coaching, I found this to be an extremely rewarding experience and still do it to this day. The enthusiasm and the unencumbered minds of those in the colleges and universities where I teach is refreshing. It can also be a challenge to my own ideas and perceptions. My students ask very difficult questions and require me to really do some soul-searching and thinking as I formulate my answers. It is interesting that many of the questions they ask are things that are obvious to me but not to them as they have never had an experience that offers a way to understand the answer in concrete terms. One of the common things I discuss with them is how to prepare for corporate life and what corporate life is really like. We talk about the need to understand culture, build relationships, and work in teams. One point I make is that, as you start out in your corporate career, you are judged mostly on your ability and very little on perception. What tends to happen, as you move up the corporate ladder and get to the higher levels of management, is that the pendulum swings dramatically to where you are judged more on perceptions rather than individual ability. I know this is not the case everywhere, but it is quite prevalent in most corporations. The students find this to be somewhat distressing because they have been taught throughout their whole academic careers to be productive contributors. We talk a lot about the fact that this is true when you're in specific jobs; however, when you start to move into the management ranks and up the chain of management, the job becomes more about influencing and perception.

One example I always offer my students is about my first job out of high school, when I worked as a carpenter. I worked with a self-educated self-taught craftsman. I learned a good deal from him, and I still use much of it to this day when doing projects around my home. The interesting thing about that job is that it was probably one of the most fulfilling I've ever had in my life. I could leave work every day and look back over my shoulder and see the fruits of my labor—whether it was a roof I recently shingled, new windows that we installed, or a new countertop in the kitchen. It gave me a personal feeling of satisfaction to know I really accomplished something of substance that day. Now, many years later, I still drive by many of those buildings I built or worked on and feel a sense of accomplishment. I haven't always found this to be true in corporate life. It seems as though the more we advance in the leadership area, the more it is about the softer things—the interactions with other people, the meetings, the trips, and the seminars. You really need to dig deep within yourself to continue to find that feeling of accomplishment and contentment. I talk a lot about this with the students and try to get them to adopt this behavior at the beginning of their careers rather than have to go through that transformation sometime later.

That is what I love about working with the university students: They really force me to think deeply when I'm having my discussions with them. Each one of us should take the time to get involved in these types of activities as it helps us to develop our ideas and a greater understanding of the important things in life. The discussions I have with the students have proven invaluable to me. The other great enjoyment I've gotten from this is following former students through their careers and watching them grow as individuals. It gives me a sense of inner peace to think I might have been able to influence them a little and help them prepare for their careers.

Bringing It All Together

I saved this final section as a place to combine all the themes and ideas presented throughout the book. The specific discussions in this chapter are designed to give you some ideas about how you might plan your personal journey. I do believe, though, that an understanding of societal changes and the ability to develop your skills in nonthreatening environments are two of the most important tools available to you as you develop your leadership style.

Throughout the book, and in this chapter, I've shared with you some of my thoughts and experiences about how to become a trusted business leader. There is no single approach or formula for success that works for everyone. However, there are many common ideas or approaches you can adopt in your personal and professional lives that prepare you to become a trusted business partner. First, it is important to believe in yourself, believe in what you can achieve, and create a set of realistic goals for yourself to help you as you develop your leadership style. Don't cast these goals in concrete; cast them in sand because as you continue your journey you will take different turns and move in different directions and you need to constantly reevaluate your personal goals to ensure they stay in alignment with where you are going. Part of becoming a trusted leader is based on circumstance as well. We develop our styles, personalities, and leadership capabilities based on our experiences throughout life.

> First, it is important to believe in yourself, believe in what you can achieve, and create a set of realistic goals for yourself to help you as you develop your leadership style.

It is important that we take the time to reflect on our experiences, their influence on us, and how we might learn from them and do things differently next time. I said on several occasions that trying to anticipate and formulate outcomes is no replacement for real-world experience. You need to be patient as you make the journey and take time to analyze and understand your experiences every day. I am often surprised when I look back over the course of a single day how much I learned from my interactions, the way I reacted to those interactions, and the way others reacted to them. Every day can be a learning experience for each of us if we open our minds and take the time to reflect on the day. The time to do that is when you're commuting home at night. Most of us have a fairly substantial commute every day and it provides a great time to sit, relax, reflect on the day, and plan for tomorrow. Use this time to your advantage, it's probably the most uninterrupted time you'll have in the course of the day.

> Every day can be a learning experience for each of us if we open our minds and take the time to reflect on the day.

There is no standard formula or menu for becoming an effective leader. It is really about first understanding your inner self, your motivations, and your desires and then combining that knowledge with a purposeful set of life experiences that help you develop your leadership style over time. I don't really believe leaders are born; I believe they are created through life's experiences and opportunities. The desire to become a leader requires commitment and dedication. It is not something you can do on a part-time basis: it is something that needs to become a part of your overall being and something you practice every day of your life. It is about challenging yourself to be the best you can be.

It is also not about being two different people: It is about being yourself and developing one style. During the course of this book, I've discussed tools to build your leadership skills and develop yourself as a leader. These tools and suggestions will only work if you take the time and make a dedicated effort to adopt the right set to match your personality and objectives. The most important thing you need to do is believe in yourself—and this is one of the hardest things to do. Allocating time for yourself and your personal development is not being selfish. Many of us tend to feel that way. It is about making yourself a better person and helping you better cope with the world and your surroundings. It will bring you closer to your family and your friends. Thinking of yourself as one person and developing one personality gives you the capability to cope with both your work and your family situations in a much more successful manner.

> I don't really believe leaders are born; I believe they are created through life's experiences and opportunities.

Start your journey today and never dwell on the past. Be excited about the future and its potential. Look back to learn from your experiences, but always look firmly forward to new ones. Don't become encumbered with the past, but learn from the experiences of the past and apply them to make a better future. Remember, as they say in racing, if you never spin out, you'll never know how fast you can go.

About the Author

A lan R. Guibord has more than 30 years of global IT management experience and is the founder and chairman of The Advisory Council (TAC). Now in its tenth year, TAC delivers a unique blend of IT expertise-as-a-service offerings that include expert advice, consulting, performance measurement, and leadership/organization development.

Prior to founding TAC, Mr. Guibord was president and chief executive officer of *Computerworld*, International Data Group's flagship weekly magazine for IT leaders. During his tenure, *Computerworld* was the only publication in its market to hold top line performance during adverse market conditions and moved from fourth position into second, based on syndicated research.

Prior to joining *Computerworld*, Mr. Guibord served as vice president and CIO of Fort James Corp., an international consumer products company with over $9 billion in sales, 28,000 employees, and more than 60 manufacturing facilities around the world. He oversaw all technology, operations, strategy, spending, and implementation, with a budget of over $250 million and a global staff of more than 1,000. He successfully led the merger of a $2 billion acquisition and executed an e-commerce strategy to accommodate retail and commercial businesses. He was a member of the corporate operating committee, capital committee, and productivity committee.

Previously, Mr. Guibord was vice president—information technology for RR Donnelley and Sons. He had global responsibility for all information technology and telecommunications and was given the challenge of redesigning the company's infrastructure and positioning it for high growth and global expansion. Before joining RR Donnelley and Sons, Mr. Guibord was chief information officer of PictureTel, Inc., positioning the business for growth from $80 million to $200 million.

Mr. Guibord has been a member of several key executive advisory boards, including Oracle and Microsoft. He sat on the advisory boards of the Grocery Manufacturers Association, the University of Illinois Chicago Center for Research in Technology, and the Chicago Library Foundation. Mr. Guibord has lectured at the University of Illinois and Northwestern University's Kellogg School of Business, University of Illinois at Chicago, and Fordham University Graduate School.

Mr. Guibord is a frequent speaker on IT leadership and organizational strategy. He is also a coach and mentor to several IT leaders. *IT Leadership Manual: Roadmap to Becoming a Trusted Business Partner* is his first book.

Index